MODERN

CIVILITY

T0058320

MODERN
CIVILITY

Etiquette for Dealing with Annoying,
Angry, and Difficult people

Cynthia W. Lett

Skyhorse Publishing

Skyhorse Publishing books may be purchased in bulk at special discounts for sales promotion, corporate gifts, fund-raising, or educational purposes. Special editions can also be created to specifications. For details, contact the Special Sales Department, Skyhorse Publishing, 307 West 36th Street, 11th Floor, New York, NY 10018 or info@skyhorsepublishing.com.

Skyhorse® and Skyhorse Publishing® are registered trademarks of Skyhorse Publishing, Inc. ®, a Delaware corporation.

www.skyhorsepublishing.com

10 9 8 7 6 5 4 3 2 1

Library of Congress Cataloging-in-Publication Data is available on file.

ISBN: 978-1-62636-412-7

Printed in China

Table of Contents

Prologue

Annoyance: a source of vexation or irritation
—-*from Merriam-Webster's Collegiate Dictionary, 10th Edition*

"That's so annoying!" "I hate it when you do that!" "She has a terrible habit of doing these things when she is around me." "He just won't stop!"

Everyday, we interact with a slew of people: significant others, children, salespeople, and strangers. Let's face it—these people have the tendency to, at any given moment, get on our nerves. Other people's behavior certainly can annoy us (and vice versa). This book is about bad habits, annoying behaviors, and how we can effectively deal with those around us who just don't seem to understand proper social etiquette.

I spent several years collecting observations, pet peeves, annoyances, and exasperations from clients, family, friends, and colleagues about ways in which people display annoying behavior. When I informed them that I was writing a book about other people's annoying behavior, I was inundated with personal grievances and irritants from everyday life. As my research continued, I realized that many people had similar complaints about the ways people behave around them, whether it is in a restaurant, in written form, or even at home. I decided that it would be crucial to offer suggestions about dealing appropriately with such irksome situations. Along the way, I also received some very insightful responses about the state of etiquette in general, and I've included these thoughts (some names have been withheld at the bequest of the submitter).

So now that we have established that people display annoying and obnoxious behavior on a daily basis (behavior that sometimes seems designed to ruin our day), we must also understand that how we react to these irksome individuals plays a key role in how we survive, and maintain sanity, in the world. Sometimes it feels as if the accused person is actually thinking, "If I do this particularly obnoxious thing, I will ruin someone's day" but, in all honesty, this is probably not the case.

We spend every day assessing the importance of other people's behavior to our happiness: "Is this going to affect my day?" "Am I really going to let this bother me?" When we spend so much time getting bothered by others, we take precious time away from achieving our daily tasks and enjoying the moment. For instance, we are home with our friends or family. It is relaxation time and we turn on the television, but we are unable to relax because so-and-so is typing loudly on the computer or what's-her-face is talking on the phone on the couch next to you. What those around us do while the television is on can be considered rude and annoying, but how we learn to react to those people's obnoxious behavior will ultimately determine how much we will enjoy our TV viewing experience.

Look at it this way: When you see mishaps and missteps on television—the guy who falls, the woman who loses her temper—the laugh track begins and lightens up the moment. If we carried our own laugh track and chose to laugh at others' bad behavior rather than allow it to grate on our nerves, our days would be happier and our relationships would be easier to maintain. It all depends on how we learn to react to annoyances around us. We can make that decision to let it roll off of us or to make a big deal about it. Wouldn't life be more fun if you just let it go? For those who sometimes just can't let it go, this book will offer solutions you should try in response to the perpetrator according to the rules of proper etiquette.

While you are reading the following chapters, I would like you to keep in mind not only the lessons you'll learn about effectively dealing with annoying people and behaviors, but also how your own behavior may affect those around you. Are you patient, empathetic, kind, tolerant, and forgiving? Or . . . are you the first one to think or say, "That's so annoying!"

Annoyance Rating System

Awfully annoying

Very annoying

Somewhat annoying

Could be annoying

Only annoying to a select few

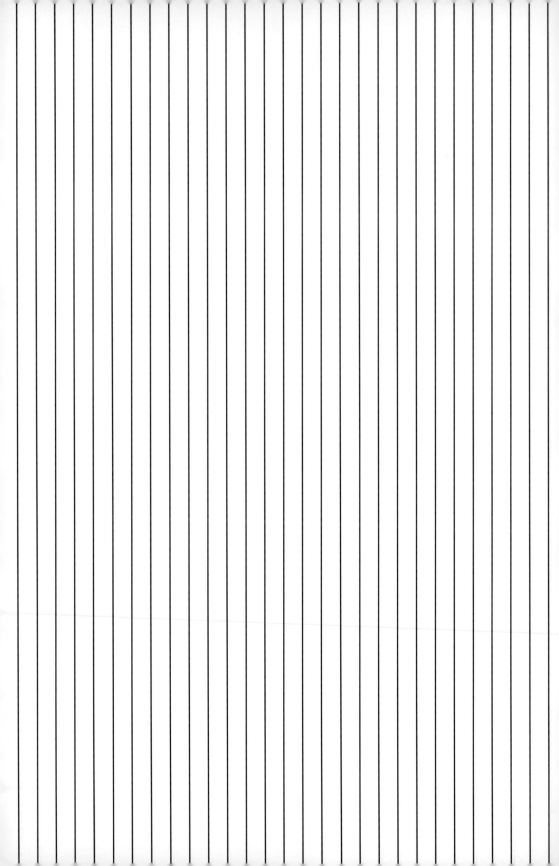

CHAPTER 1

SIGNIFICANT OTHERS AND CHILDREN

In our home—our sanctuary—we sometimes encounter the source of our greatest annoyance: our family and significant others. Almost everyone I talked with who is or was married or in a partner-ship had a spousal bad-behavioral issue to share. Some didn't stop with just their significant others and included their children, extended family, and neighbors in their examples. Some contributors shared so many that I was left wondering if anything could make them truly happy at home. Many of the grievances centered on the television—a major point of contention. The rest covered the kitchen, the laundry, the housework, and the bedroom (for the sake of good taste, I am not including the bedroom examples in this book—I'll leave those to the sex therapists). Learning what can be annoying in the home and then finding out how to react to these situations will hopefully help make domestic life more blissful.

Husbands and Boyfriends

"My husband smokes!" "My husband leaves the toilet seat up!" "My husband has a messy desk!" Many women find bothersome behavior emanating from their male companions. Whether the annoyance is about the kitchen, bathroom, laundry, bodily functions, bedroom, or communication (or lack of it), husbands and boyfriends were a major source of contention for the women I spoke to.

The Kitchen

Key Complaints

Husbands make too many messes.

Dirty dishes are left on the counter.

Husbands don't do dishes, period.

In many households, the kitchen is the woman's domain. Fortunately there is a trend toward capable men who love to cook and do it well. Now, even children get into chef mode and help out with meals on a regular basis. However, the majority of kitchens still seem to be run by the woman of the house, giving rise to a plethora of complaints about what others (primarily husbands) do in the kitchen. The top annoying behaviors revolve around cleanliness, food, and simple presence in the kitchen.

"My husband drinks out of the milk or juice carton."

—*Complaint from many annoyed wives*

Whenever hygiene is concerned, I suggest that rules of etiquette become part of the rules of the house. Drinking directly from any carton is terribly unsanitary. *The Solution:* Because you live with him, suggest that no one wants to drink the remaining contents of the carton when his germs have been slobbered all over the flap. If he doesn't amend his bad behavior, perhaps it's time for him to buy his own carton of milk. That way, he can do what he wants while you enjoy a germ-free container.

"My husband or kid leaves about one half inch of juice in the container and puts it back in fridge so he doesn't have to make more."

—Annoyance from a wife and mother

The Solution: A simple way to deal with this gripe is to leave the juice container in the fridge and, when you are asked to make more, tell the culprit that it is now his responsibility because they want more juice. You can choose to be the servant (and continue to be annoyed with this behavior) or you can train your family to serve themselves.

"I am gone all day and come home and my husband says he is starving, like he couldn't feed himself?"

—Barbara in Los Angeles, CA

Here's an idea: Ask him what is for dinner. After all, it has been a tough day for you, too. If you and your significant other have taxing work schedules, and neither of you enjoy cooking, establish a weekly meal plan, alternating who cooks each day of the week. That way, no one feels burdened with all the cooking, and no one has real reason to become annoyed.

What is it About Coffee?

"Cleaning up after my husband's coffee mess
[is frustrating]."
—*Carol Landry from New Mexico*

"There is no coffee left because my husband drank
it all."
—*Numerous wives*

These complaints stem from laziness, self-absorption, and lack of respect. ***The Solution:*** Set guidelines for members of your household when it comes to taking responsibility for their own messes and for thinking of others. Model the behavior you would like others in the house to use. Employ positive reinforcement when your husband or boyfriend remembers to clean up the coffee grinds or brew a fresh pot of joe. If you praise him and let him know how much you appreciate it, hopefully you will see repeated attempts to do the right thing—and experience less annoyance on your part.

Emptying the Trash

"My husband will not take out the trash."
—*Wives across the country*

When it comes to chores like taking the trash out and moving the newspapers to the recycle bin, usually these will get accomplished without nagging if you can remember to compliment him when he remembers to do these chores. It is a matter of training. We all remember what it takes to get praise from those we love.

Avoid the Annoyance: Easy Ways to Get Your Husband to Take Out the Trash

1. Place acceptable footwear by the door. You need shoes to take the trash out. By placing slip-on shoes close to the door where the trash goes out, it may be easier to accomplish.
2. Have the appropriate outerwear accessible for trash days. If it is cold outside, who wants to go out? A sweater or jacket near the door could also encourage him.
3. Make it fun! Work as a team: One person throws out the trash while the other deals with the recyclables. Or make it a competition: See who can take it out the fastest or who empties more trash than the other.
4. Split the load. Set up a weekly schedule for trash removal and stick to your end of the deal.
5. Always say "thank you." Positive reinforcement encourages repeated actions.

Snoring

Key Complaints

My husband snores!

My wife snores!

"I'm annoyed with my wife making me sleep in the den because I snore."

—*Roger O'Donnell of California*

The Solution: Don't be annoyed; be proactive! This is such a common grumble among couples. Though snoring grates on our nerves and causes sleeplessness on the part of the bed partner, remember: It is not done on purpose and is probably a health problem that needs medical attention. Would you make your partner sleep on the couch if he had a broken arm? Instead of being annoyed, spend some time together trying to figure out why the snoring is happening and what, if anything, can make it stop. Perhaps all that's needed is a different sleep position, new pillow, nose strips, or drinking more water during the day. Nasal strips really do work (at least at our house). So does medical treatment. Remember that the snorer isn't getting quality sleep either so solving this should be a team effort. We all hate to have our sleep interrupted. So, instead of stewing in frustration, make a doctor's appointment for the snorer. You will both get a better (and less frustrated) night's sleep.

Doing the Laundry

"My husband always takes off his dirty clothes and leaves them in front of the basement door—which is right in between the dining area and the living room."

—*A flustered wife*

The Solution: Instead of getting annoyed, the next time you have guests coming to the house, don't clean this up but be sure to point out to them that your husband believes this is where laundry belongs in your house. Though I am only partly kidding with this suggestion, if he knew that guests would see his mess, he would probably make sure it was put away before they came again. And the next time he puts things where they belong, make a big deal about it and let him know how much you appreciate his help in keeping the house tidy.

"My husband leaves his clothes on the floor *next* to the laundry basket!"

—*Anonymous wife*

Maybe he doesn't know what the basket's purpose is. ***The Solution:*** Don't just assume your significant other is going to know what to do with everything in the house. Just give him a friendly reminder that clothes should be placed into the laundry basket. Asking him to place his clothes in the basket once should take care of the problem. If not, just don't wash the clothes that aren't in the basket. When he has nothing clean left to wear, inform him that you will only wash the clothes that make their way into the appropriate basket. See? No need to get annoyed—after all, at least *your* clothes are getting washed.

The Art of Communication

> "My husband is always saying 'You never told me that!'"
>> —*Melanie R. of Leesburg, VA*

Did you know that sometimes we all say things to other people in our own minds but don't actually verbalize our thoughts out loud? Some of the blame for believing that others are not listening falls upon ourselves for not actually talking. Maybe you think you heard yourself say to your husband, "My friend Jane is coming for dinner tonight" but you didn't get any response. Well, did you ask for a response? ***The Solution:*** The best way to know that you have been heard, and to escape the annoyance with your husband's lack of communication, is to ask for feedback. Try, "Are you happy about that?" or "Can you help me get ready?" If he didn't hear what you said, he will most likely ask what you are talking about (because your question didn't make sense). This is a great time to clarify what you said and feel secure that he is listening.

Similarly, many wives become exceedingly annoyed when their husbands do not listen to them at all. ***The Solution:*** If we want someone to really listen to us, it is essential to make direct contact with that person. This could be eye-to-eye connection or a touch on the arm. I have found that if we are focused on the person who is speaking, we listen better. Another tactic that works is asking him to listen. You could say, "Can I tell you something?" or "Honey, I need to tell you about our plans this afternoon." Then wait for a reaction. If one doesn't come, repeat yourself. If you follow these simple suggestions, you'll be more likely to come away from these difficult communication issues less perturbed and more satisfied.

Oh, Dear: Bonus Annoyances Regarding Communication with Our Husbands

"My husband never admits that he did anything that I wouldn't like."

—*Katie B. from Burlington, VT*

"My husband never admits he's wrong."

—*M. from New York, NY*

"[I'm annoyed] when my husband gets mad and starts cussing just because something did not go like he wants it to."

—*Kyra from San Francisco, CA*

"My husband says 'hold on' every time I say anything."

—*M.C. from Frederick, MD*

Miscellaneous Annoyances

These are additional situations that show either bad behavior or annoying actions on behalf of male significant others. While some are more humorous than others, it is important to remember that how we respond to each annoyance plays a key part in our ability to stave off frustration with the people closest to us.

"My husband [is] constantly belching and farting."

—*Anne in Rhode Island*

This actually sounds like a medical problem. The human body isn't supposed to play a nonstop symphony. *The Solution:* Ask him to talk to his doctor. Or, supply some anti-gas tablets to see if they work for him.

> "My husband leaves used dental floss
> on the kitchen counter."
>
> —*Disgusted wife*

Yuck! This is certainly gross and also a germ issue. *The Solution:* Ask him to pick it up and put it into the trash, explaining that his germs are being transmitted to the counter where food is prepared. Hopefully this should give him the hint that he needs to take things one step further and throw his floss away.

> "[I'm annoyed] when my husband gets a new roll of toilet
> paper and sets it on the sink. . . . Actually putting it on the
> roller is way too difficult! Way too complicated!"
>
> —*Linda E. from Miami Beach, FL*

The Solution: Encourage him to follow through. Praise him the next time he puts the toilet paper roll on the dispenser. He will more likely repeat the action if he knows you notice his efforts. If praise doesn't seem to do the trick, just remember that sometimes we just have to follow some people and complete what they don't do for themselves.

> "I could scream when my husband cleans out the car and
> piles everything on the kitchen table I have just cleaned."
>
> —*Beatrice P. of San Juan, Puerto Rico*

I would say he probably is grateful to you for clearing off a place on the table for him to put the junk. *The Solution:* Before you even start to get annoyed, ask him to take all the things from the car to a designated spot. Giving him good directions will clear up this problem, and your desire to scream, quickly.

> "My husband of twenty years still doesn't
> know what to buy for me."
>
> —*Robin M. of New York City*

Here's my humble suggestion: Understand that, after twenty years of failed present-giving attempts, he will never know what to buy for you so it will be up to you to tell him. I promise he will find great relief when you do—and you'll actually get something you want. See? Everyone wins with this point.

> "My husband does not help me clean the house."
>
> —*Many, many wives*

Though it's true that women would love to have their men automatically start dusting, mopping, and cleaning the bathrooms, it most likely won't happen if there isn't a "what's in it for me?" reward. ***The Solution:*** Think of a good reason—maybe a "prize" to be won—why he would be more than willing to pitch in and help clean the house. Most of the time, just a heartfelt "thank you" and the recognition of a job well done will be enough for him. However, if you don't think that will be incentive enough, you can think of what would entice cooperation from him on your own.

> "[It's frustrating] when husbands/boyfriends go to the
> grocery store for their wives/girlfriends and then have to
> call to find out what it is they need."
>
> — *Various wives and girlfriends*

Don't fret, ladies. He is only calling because he wants to please you—so there is no need to get annoyed with this thoughtful gesture. He is trying to avoid your annoyed or angry response if he comes home with the wrong orange juice or cheese or cookies. Even in my house, with a detailed list in hand, calling from the grocery store occurs.

"[I become very annoyed] when husbands think they are perfect and believe that we women are always wrong."

—*Disgruntled wives*

First, don't take it personally. In my experience, I've actually come to believe that husbands are intimidated by their wives, and their "I am perfect" response is a defense to feeling incredibly inferior. And let's face it: They are right. We can be intimidating. So just smile and nod and know that you still have the upper hand.

"[I tire of] listening to my husband's stories over and over."

—*One annoyed wife*

Yes, listening to the same story for years and years can be both boring and annoying. ***The Solution:*** A gentle reminder that you know the story will help him remember that he has already shared it. If he is telling an old story to new people, join in and be as enthusiastic as he is with it. Make it fun and perhaps you'll find something new about his latest version that you never knew before.

Wives and Girlfriends

Don't be confused: Men also find annoying behavior in their wives and girlfriends. Though most of the men I spoke to did not necessarily place their complaints about their significant others in set "domestic" categories, they did voice frustrations about the actions (or inactions) their wives and girlfriends take.

"My wife tries to keep me busy, but I am retired and do not want to do anything."

—*Retired husband*

Retirement is certainly a transition for everyone in the household, not just for the retiree. Studies have shown that active retirees live longer and healthier than those who prefer to do nothing special. Your wife is just trying to keep you around longer. *The Solution:* Maybe you can actively seek out something that excites you to help keep you busy. That way, your wife will be happy to see you active and you'll be doing something you thoroughly enjoy. Take the proactive approach and your frustration will fly the coop.

> "[I'm annoyed by] my girlfriend who refuses to promptly put things back where she got them from. Anything from leaving the milk on the counter to the phone book left open on the table. Arrrghhh!"
>
> —*Paul Miller of Pennsylvania*

It sounds like she has a lot on her mind and forgets to follow through. *The Solution:* Provide her with gentle reminders that will help her remember. Perhaps she never grew up in an environment where cleaning up after oneself was important. You could also share how much it bothers you and why. If we know we are bothering someone we care about, we tend to try to make our behavior more acceptable.

> "My wife gives my clothes to Goodwill without telling me."
>
> —*Bill P. of Maine*

A good solution to this problem would be to pick out what needs to be given away together so you can have some control and she can tell you why she thinks something should go. Ask her to tell you before she makes a run to Goodwill. If you become part of the donation process, not only will your wife be happy to share the responsibility but you will not lose precious possessions.

> "My wife has gotten really, really fat."
>
> —*Anonymous frustrated husband*

Listen to this: Experts say that there is always a reason why some-one gains weight after marriage. To help your wife tackle any weight issues, you first need to find out the reason behind the weight gain. The best approach is to participate with her in making positive changes to her lifestyle. Most men who complain about their wives usually have gained some weight themselves. Make it a healthy change rather than accusing her of "letting herself go." Whatever you do, try not to become annoyed with this (for the better of both of you). I would venture to say that she is just as disturbed by the weight gain as you are but is also too embarrassed to discuss it.

"My wife hides the remote for the TV."

—Mark Miller of Mississippi

There is a reason why she hides the remote. Could it be that you play with it too much while she is trying to watch something? ***The Solution:*** Instead of becoming annoyed, the proper response to the missing remote would be to ask her why she hid the remote and then what would prompt her to find it and give it back to you? This situation calls for compromise and a little understanding on both sides.

"My wife makes a big deal out of all of our anniversaries."

—Husbands around the country

Well, guys, anniversaries celebrate happy occasions and she is hop-ing that they mean the same to you. She makes a big deal of them because they are important milestones in your relationship. Suggestion: Start making a big deal out of them too—just for one year—and you will see why it is worth your effort.

"My wife never fills up the gasoline tank in the car."

—Husbands who like to drive

There are many women who separate chores into "his" and "hers" in their mind. If she is the one who always fixes dinner or cleans the house or takes care of the grocery shopping, then she has determined hers. Yet, that doesn't mean she should just assume that you know your duty in the household. *The Solution:* Ask her if she would like for you to fill the gas tank in the car as one of your chores. If she says yes, then you have your reason why she doesn't fill it promptly as you do. If she says no, tell her that you would like for her to take care of it occasionally, and then give her gentle reminders.

"My wife is always wearing my clothes."

—*Corby C.*

Many women are quite comfortable in the styles that their men wear and, if you are bigger than she, the loose fit that men's clothing offers. She doesn't want to purchase her own because yours is readily accessible. *The Solution:* Why not designate a shirt or two as hers to wear? Or, if you really feel frustrated with this, just tell her that you like your clothes and that you'd prefer if she bought some comfortable clothes for herself. It's not reasonable to become annoyed with this behavior if you haven't told her how you feel.

"My wife won't do my laundry."

—*Disgruntled husbands*

This doesn't really qualify as an annoying habit, but the solution is still simple. Talk with your wife about why she won't do your laundry. If it is because she doesn't have the time, but she is still managing to get *her* clothes washed and dried, then that is something you can contest with her. If, on the other hand, she can't stand that your clothes are so filthy, then ask her to teach you how to wash them. Most spouses are inclined not to do things for their significant other because it is demanded rather than requested. Remember the bottom line of good etiquette is making requests rather than demands. In most cases a sweet request with a reward at the end will change a reluctant spouse's behavior and alleviate any frustration on your part.

"My girlfriend starts a project and expects me to finish it."

—Annoyed boyfriend

Many people, not just women, get enthusiastic about starting a new project and then, once into it, realize they are in over their head. They want the finished product, but don't have the skills, or the drive, to complete it on their own. She may be relying on you because you have the skills she lacks. ***The Solution:*** Have a conversation with her when she begins a new project to see if she has the expectation that you will complete it if she cannot. If she says yes, you have the option at that point to inform her whether you will or won't meet that expectation. There is no written rule that you must pick up her slack—you just need to be straightforward about it and then it won't be an annoyance in the future.

"My wife won't order dessert, but eats all of mine."

—Hungry husbands

Here's a tip: What you need to understand, guys, is that women don't want to look like they want dessert, especially if they are watching their weight, but the temptation is often stronger than will power when the dessert comes to the table. She then relies on your goodwill to share your plate. You don't really mind, do you? Well, if you mind, make sure you tell her after the meal and also offer to buy her a dessert the next time you are out. And, make sure she understands that you won't judge her for her sweet tooth.

Funny Husband Annoyance of the Day

"My wife won't scale fish."

—Robert L.

Well neither will I, especially if there is a fish scaling expert like you around to do a stellar job at it, which I guarantee I couldn't do. Don't expect your significant other to be willing to do things outside of her comfort zone—if she doesn't want to cut the scales off a dead fish, I think you can cut her some slack here and forget the frustration.

Children

> "My pet peeve about kids is that they exist at all!"
> —*William Z. from Santa Barbara, California*

I received an astoundingly large number of complaints about kids. These are from the parents about their own kids and everyone else about everyone else's kids. Some were from kids about other kids. There is a definite focus to these complaints. Some people just don't like kids in general, so I can't hope to instill tolerance and acceptance in them. However, there are several common forms of dislike when it comes to kids' behavior. Everyone dislikes out of control children. Everyone dislikes people, and especially children, who are loud, dirty, foul mouthed, and spoiled. What is interesting, though, is that so many of the complaints were about the parents and how they raised their children. Children are not born slobs, disrespectful, out of control, loud, bored, or spoiled. Someone must have allowed or encouraged these traits. Many of these annoyances are about parents shirking their responsibility to raise well-mannered kids.

We typically judge children based upon our own children, if we have them. If we don't have our own, we judge ill-mannered children against the best-behaved, best-dressed, and smartest child we've ever met. Very few parents admit that they struggle with parenting. Parents tend to see only the best behaviors of their children and revel in the positive comments they receive from others. Parents compare their kids to the kids of other parents. "I would never let my child do that!" is a common exclamation I hear from parents whose kids are the worst behaved of all. Or, I sometimes hear exasperated parents say, "I just can't control him!" The problem I see is that parents just don't know what to do to change unacceptable behavior. It has been pointed out that parents don't understand that proper conduct in a child starts at birth. Babies watch the adults around them. They listen to the words spoken and tones of voice used. They watch body language and mimic everything they see. What they see the most are the parents' and siblings' demeanor. They hear their words. They want to be just like them. A child's attitude all starts with the parents. You cannot expect good behavior to come from a child who has never witnessed it from those he mimics. Whether in a restaurant, at the grocery store, or in your own home, it is vital to learn how to effectively react to the annoyances stemming from a child's bad behavior.

Restaurants

I can certainly understand why the most prevalent complaint about annoying children focuses on their loud, out of control behavior in restaurants.

> "Kids who scream in restaurants and parents who don't stop them ruin everyone's meal. I blame the parents for allowing it."
>
> —*Mitchell Robins from Colorado*

People who don't control their kids in restaurants are showing their lack of concern for their fellow diners. I blame it on a lack of discipline on the parents' part, who, in turn, don't know how to discipline their children to behave appropriately. When I watch parents with out of control kids, I often see adults who are tired, exasperated, and flus- tered—parents who don't know how to respond in the correct manner. When our son was quite small and had a breakdown in a public place, particularly in restaurants and stores, it took only seconds for us to take him outside until he calmed down. If it seemed that he couldn't settle down, we all went home. We believed that we had no right to interrupt and annoy other people who were having a meal and paying for the experience of a restaurant dinner. It was just a stage in our lives as parents. We knew that we wouldn't be interrupting meals forever. So how can you, as an observer to this screaming child, get your annoyance under control? It's simple. The best reaction is to stay calm and approach the parents' table. You might say something like, "You have beautiful children but right now their behavior is disrupting our meal. I know you wouldn't mind bringing them under control so that you can enjoy your meal as well." Of course, use your own words. The point of this is not to attack them for their child's indiscretion but to empathize and show your concern for them as well as yourself. If a gentle approach doesn't work, you have every right to share your concern with the management and leave the solution up to them.

On another note, have you seen a well-behaved, quiet, thoughtful child sitting at a restaurant table, eating with proper manners? I venture to say you have, but you haven't directly noticed him. He doesn't stand out because he isn't interrupting your meal. He isn't annoying you. As you walked out, did you compliment the child or his parents on how delightful it was to dine in the same restaurant as them that evening? It would be rare if you did. This is exactly why you should do it. When you observe someone doing something right, acknowledge the good behavior. Compliments go a long way in encouraging children (and even adults) to behave properly again. There is power in positive words, so use them whenever you can!

A Meltdown

> "I become annoyed with the lack of patience and assistance from others when my autistic son has an outburst."
>
> —*Barbara from Chicago, IL*

Barbara said that taking her son to the grocery store or to a fast-food restaurant is unavoidable at times. Sometimes she has difficulty with his emotional outbursts and meltdowns when the world around him becomes too intense or confusing. Often, he will suddenly scream or flail about. This is her reality with her child and all she wants is a little patience and understanding. Instead, she is the recipient of dirty looks, snide comments, complaints to the manager, and general disdain from those around them.

Much of our reaction to inappropriate or ill-mannered behavior from others comes from our lack of understanding or our unwillingness to empathize. *The Solution:* If you see a child having a meltdown and a distraught parent trying to handle it, think about if you were in that situation and how much you would appreciate a kind word or a little assistance. Barbara says that if someone would just ask if they can carry something for her, or hold the door open or express their willingness to help if needed, her struggle with her son's outbursts would be more quickly resolved and less disruptive and she wouldn't feel like she is the worst mother. Showing a little empathy will not only help resolve the situation, but will also channel your annoyance into a positive outlet.

Appearance of Children

"It's annoying to see nicely dressed parents with poorly dressed kids."

—*Fashion savvy people*

This scenario generally occurs when well-dressed, well-mannered parents are at the stage when they are teaching their children to dress themselves. Picking out clothes for the child normally stops in most households when the child reaches age eight or nine. It would be a great favor to the children, however, if the parents had set standards and expectations for the child's wardrobe when leaving the house so that the general public wouldn't assume they don't care about their children's presentation. *The Solution:* Don't be so quick to judge the well-groomed parents when you see sloppy kids with them. It was probably one of those "pick your battle" situations in their home that day.

"I'm annoyed by women who dress in name brands while their kids wear junk."

—*Anonymous*

I venture to say that this pet peeve came from someone who doesn't have his own children or someone to whom money is no object. I actually understand the reasoning for this since my children grew, and continue to grow, quickly, right out of the brand-name clothes we just bought last month. In the name of thriftiness and good sense, parents should ignore labels until the child will be able to wear the item for at least one year without growing out of it. The key to getting away with this kind of thriftiness is buying inexpensive but sturdy clothes so they don't look like rags after two washes.

> "I'm annoyed with kids wearing pants that
> show their underwear."
>
> —*Anonymous adults*

I was driving today and noticed on the sidewalk a teenage boy with jeans on, the waist around the middle of his thighs and crotch at his knees. He was on a manual scooter and having great difficulty maneuvering it with the restriction of his pants on his legs. His underwear was blue, which was entirely too much information, and he looked absolutely ridiculous to this child of the 1970s. Of course, have you seen the clothes coming back into style that mimic the ones we wore then? Oh my God! How could we? At least no one knew what color our underwear was. **The Solution:** Just shake it off. You can't go around trying to change everyone's sense of fashion. Just chuckle and move on. But if *you* have kids that age, do us all a favor and don't let them dress that way!

Out at the Store

> "I hate it when I see kids running all over a store
> without parental supervision."
>
> —*Kim B. from Albuquerque, New Mexico*

The Solution: Whenever I'm in a store and encounter a child without a parent in tow, I stop and ask the child where his mom or dad is. If he says they are close by, I suggest that they are looking for him and he should go find them. I have found a couple of times I asked, the answer was, "I don't know." Then I find a store manager and turn the child over to her. Don't assume the child or the parent is doing something to annoy you. It may be that either one is just lost.

"I'm frustrated with people who bring their screaming kids shopping and then yell at them and spank them for screaming. Let's face it: Did you want to go shopping all day when you were three years old? Get a babysitter. I didn't bring my kid, so I don't want to hear yours!"

—*Anonymous parent*

It is understandable that this would annoy certain parents (especially those who make it a rule not to bring their young children on long shopping ventures), but sometimes a babysitter is not an option. *The Solution:* Just grin and bear it. We cannot reasonably expect children to behave all the time. If the child's behavior is really unnerving you, I suggest you leave the store and continue your shopping elsewhere.

Around the House

"I am especially annoyed when my kids refuse to go to bed."

—*Many parents*

The Solution: Let them stay awake but in their own rooms, away from the rest of the family and away from their television and video games. Boredom will put them to sleep faster than your nagging and then you won't have to be annoyed with their insubordination at bedtime.

"It's so annoying when the kids bring down glasses that have obviously sat in their rooms for a few days—ewww!"

—*Kimberly S. from Los Angeles, California*

I have a perfect fix for this one—no glasses or food allowed in their rooms anymore. Not only is it unsanitary (crumbs and drips) but accidents happen and homework can get drenched. You have power over this problem so don't let it annoy you. Just make a rule and stick to it. There, problem solved.

> "I live in a house with my mom, my five kids, and my husband, and the thing that drives me nuts about it is that no one puts things away when they are done with them. Then they scream, 'Mom where's my whatever?' 'I don't know where it is. . . . It's wherever you left it.'"
>
> —*Karen from Louisiana*

You don't have to have five children to have this frustration in your home. One is all it takes. ***The Solution:*** Sit the children down and explain that everything has a place and it is their responsibility to keep things in order. (I know you are laughing out loud at this point but bear with me.) Then, help them organize their things in labeled storage places that are easily reachable for them. As they learn the skill of putting things away, there needs to be a reward. It could be kudos from you and their father or a special treat. You will no longer be the chief detective in relation to their belongings, they will learn some important life skills, and your annoyance level will drastically decrease.

Electronics

> "It's annoying when I see kids with their heads in handheld video games all day long!"
>
> —*Anonymous*

The Solution: If these are your children, then you have the power to take the game away or limit its use. If this applies to other kids, be grateful they are quiet and not getting into trouble. You may not have control over the amount of game time these children are eating up, but is it really worth getting annoyed about?

"Kids with their twenty-four-hour text messaging are
extremely annoying."

—*Anonymous parent*

Text messaging has taken the place of face-to-face communication
in many teens' lives. ***The Solution:*** If your children are still living at
home, and you are still paying the bill for the phone, you have the
power to determine how much and how long they text. Don't enable
the problem—rather, solve it and be done with it.

Parents and Their Children

Key Complaints

"My kids are always talking or arguing
when I'm on the phone."

"My kids are always interrupting."

"My kids don't listen to me."

"I'm annoyed with parents who don't come see their kids'

school performances."

Even the most loving parents are bound to become annoyed
with their children's bad behavior at times. But sometimes, parents
hold lofty expectations for their children and become annoyed for
things that they cannot directly control. Here are some legitimate
(and irrational) annoyances that parents have of their children.

"It's quite frustrating when my kids sit among a pile of
games and toys and complain they have nothing to do!"

—*Anonymous parent*

Sometimes kids are tired of the old way of playing with their toys if
they have had them for a while. ***The Solution:*** Why not be creative and

show them some new ways of engaging with their toys? That should keep them busy and you less flustered.

> "Kids who don't do well in school while parents are paying their way are extremely annoying."
>
> —*Various college parents*

I believe these parents are missing the point. Many children have learning difficulties that have not been diagnosed or accommodated. ***The Solution:*** Instead of complaining about what the child isn't doing right, a team effort between the teacher, counselor, and parents to figure out what it would take to help the child learn better would solve the problem. Most kids want to do well but don't have the skills needed to accomplish their goals and their parents' expectations. Help provide the child with resources to enable him to succeed in school.

> "My kids are not keeping in touch with us as much as we would like."
>
> —*Empty nesters*

Remember: If you find not being with your children is a problem, imagine what your child might be feeling. Perhaps a day trip (nothing too time consuming for the children who are busy with their own lives) would keep the connection. E-mails help with day-to-day connecting and there is still the old-fashioned but very effective hand-written letter. Kids still model their parents' gestures so if you make the effort, at some point it will be returned.

> "The fact that my kids ignore that I am aging is annoying."
>
> —*One disgruntled parent*

Really? Unless your kids truly understand that they too are aging, I venture to say that this complaint will be unresolved. When they feel the first pains, they will suddenly understand what you and all of us aging parents are feeling. So wait a couple of years and then see if you can't have a talk with them about how it makes you feel when they ignore your aging process.

"[I hate it] when my kids act out in public because they know it's harder [for me] to say no."

—*Mary from Washington, D.C.*

We all hate it when kids act out in public because it is often loud and disruptive. My suggestion is to set the ground rules before leaving home. Even if you have to repeat yourself for years, every time you leave home explain your expectations for the outing and the reward for good behavior. After a while, the rewards can be reduced and eliminated because the good behavior will be the child's common behavior and the rest of us will have a quieter world in which to move. This is one situation where your proactive reasoning will win over your feelings of annoyance and manipulation.

Miscellaneous Annoyances

"Grandparents who brag about their grandkids annoy me."

—*Anonymous people*

This surprised me, but many people's annoyances were about grandparents and having to listen to their bragging. When a grandparent brags, they are showing off their pride—not in just their grandkids, but actually in their children who are the parents. It is like hearing "I did a good job in my parenting because my kids have amazing kids." ***The Solution:*** If you know a grandparent, give him a chance to talk about a subject that is important to him. You should ask how his grandchildren are and then listen. After a few minutes of bragging, validate his enthusiasm by saying how lucky the children are to have him as a grandparent—and then change the subject. You will be allowing him the freedom of expression and also providing yourself with a way out of the bragging-rights saga.

"[I'm annoyed by] kids who don't send thank you notes
for gifts received."

—*Jeannie from Madison, Wisconsin*

Not receiving a thank you or acknowledgment for a gift sent is a common complaint. You spent the time and effort to find something you think the person would like and sent it but then—no response. Did he get it? Did he like it? Does he appreciate the effort you made? All of these are the questions at hand. ***The Solution:*** I suggest that the giver make a phone call to make sure he received it. If he did, and he still doesn't thank you for it, you can always choose not to send a gift for the next occasion. Thank you notes are the easiest notes to write. Three lines are all you need: "Dear Grandma, Thank you for the great game. I am going to have a lot of fun playing it. I hope we can see you soon. Love, Bobby." The first line is the thank you for what was given. The second line is what you will do with it, and the third is a positive action. So simple and so appreciated.

"I get annoyed with people who expect me to babysit
their kids where I work."

—*Busy coworker*

Here is a situation where you are the one in power. If you cannot devote the time to watch your coworkers' children, a comment such as, "I wish I could but I am swamped with the budget report and am on deadline. As a matter of fact, I was just looking for a quiet place to finish this up" will politely let them know that you aren't being paid as their at-work nanny.

"Kids bickering, fighting, and yelling at each other grate
on my last nerve."

—*Gerry Paul P. from California*

This is a sentiment shared by any parent of siblings. A wise man told me once to take yourself out of the fray if you are sure there won't be bloodshed. Kids need to learn how to handle disagreements.

The Solution: Instruct the children to talk quietly—on a procedure that works—and then let them practice the skill when they are combative. Actively participating in conflict mediation with any child will not only help the child later on in life but will help bring down your blood pressure.

> "I'm always embarrassed when my children tell my age on my birthday."
>
> —*C. LaBlanc from Portland, Maine*

When we are around young people, there are certain givens that we come to expect regarding the information they may divulge. However, we do hope they will keep our secrets. A good etiquette rule is to keep your promises and other peoples' secrets. So listen up because this could be an important lesson for your kids. Of course my son thinks I am twenty-nine years old (and I always will be in my mind). I am sure as his subtracting skills get better he will have a eureka moment and figure it out. But I only celebrate anniversaries of my twenty-ninth birthday, so I am not one to give advice on this topic. If you are really sensitive about your age, then don't make it known to your child until he is old enough to also understand that it is polite to respect others' wishes in regards to disclosing our age.

> "People picking on little kids is my pet peeve."
>
> —*Leroy K. from Nashville, TN*

Now really, how much of a bully can you be to pick on a child if you are an adult? ***The Solution:*** If you see this, it is your responsibility to society to say something to the adult or to alert authorities if you feel you could be threatened. No child should have to defend himself from an adult's attack. Don't just get annoyed—get involved!

Funny Acts of Annoyance (Adults vs. Children)

> "Kids thinking they know it all."
>
> —*Joelle M. from Utah*

"Knowing kids think the 80s is ancient history."

—*Anonymous*

It's true that children can be a never-ending source of frustration for everyone—not just the parents. Many told me that their frustrations with kids are really quite focused. They revolve around the way children look, sound, walk, sit, talk, stand, interact with others, fight, sing, and generally exist. My belief is that a child who has been taught and practices proper manners is a joy to be around—sometimes moreso than an adult. Did you know that children who display proper etiquette and respect for others and themselves are more often mentored by influential adults? Their future possibilities are greater and brighter because adults who can help them genuinely want to be around them.

Author's Note: My Personal List of Annoying Behaviors in Respect to Children and Their Parents

- Seeing kids in cars without seat belts on. I fear for their safety and question their parents' judgment.
- Boys with the crotch of their pants at their knees.
- Girls with pants so tight they look painted on—especially when they don't have a body to support such revelation.
- Parents who can't control their temper against their children in public.
- Parents who have abdicated their responsibility by leaving their homes and their children fatherless or motherless.
- Erectile dysfunction commercials when kids are watching TV. I share this one with a slew of other disgruntled watchers of commercials not appropriate during hours when children are awake.
- Parents who don't support their kids' activities. Many don't attend anything at their kids' school. It only hurts the child who wants his parents to be proud of his accomplishments.

Living with people we love is a constant give-and-take, and compromising isn't always easy. When the small annoyances start clouding our acceptance of others, step back and take a deep breath. Know that, though you might find certain behaviors you dislike in the ones you are closest to, you do still love them and owe it to both them and yourself to practice some patience and to learn to react rationally to their idiosyncrasies.

Notes

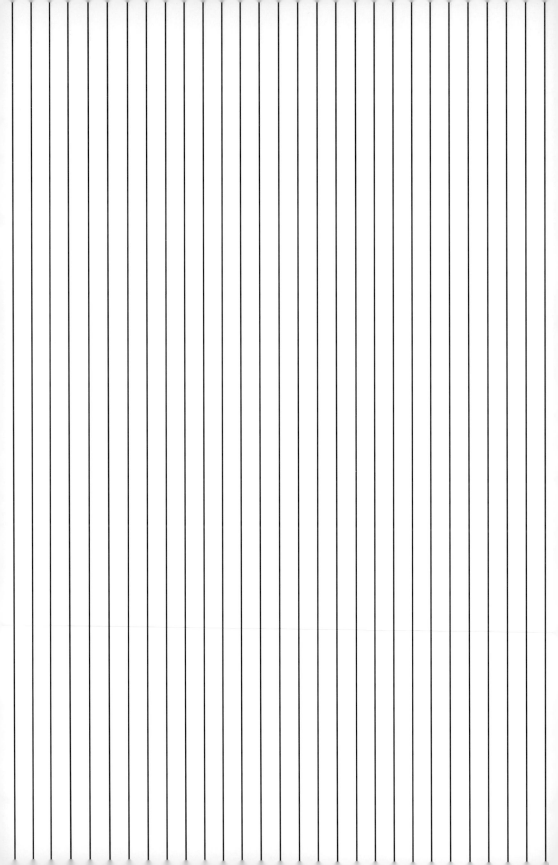

CHAPTER 2

EATING WITH OTHERS

Eating: Everyone must do it to survive but the ways in which people interact with food (both in private and in public) can sometimes be less than appealing to an outside observer. During my research, I received a string of annoyances revolving around food, its consumption, restaurant etiquette, and table manners. It seems apparent that we (the general public) wouldn't have any complaints about dining in or out with other people if the other people had already mastered basic table manners. But who actually teaches table manners anymore? Of course etiquette experts do. Mothers and fathers who know these manners try to instill them in their children. Teachers in elementary schools attempt to help children learn the proper eating etiquette. My feeling is that the media plays a big part in the lack of dining manners we observe today. Every day we watch TV shows that display boorish table manners. Sloppiness at the table doesn't seem to offend the directors of movies or television shows. In this case, the public models the actors' bad manners and believes it is ok—after all, it is on TV.

It's important to remember that what you show others at the table is in direct relation to the impression they will have about every part of your relationship with them. If you know how to hold your utensils and pass the bread, they may think that you are a savvy individual. Eating with others isn't supposed to be necessarily about the food. It is about relationship building. This is your chance to have a captive audience for your wit and wisdom and any distraction your table manners offer will take away from the positive impression you are trying to make.

We notice bad manners much more often than we notice good ones. Bad manners are a distraction and an annoyance. Knowing which fork to use and how to eat your bread shows respect for others as well as for yourself—and gives your eating companion no reason to become annoyed with your behavior. This chapter is full of the annoyances that we have when encountering fellow diners who have never learned or don't seem to care about good table manners. Furthermore, this chapter is concerned with not only how people eat but also where and what they eat.

Hearing Others Eat

Smacking, slurping, burping, chewing, chomping, and crunching. By far the most common annoyance is the sound of others eating. Sometimes, hearing others chew their food sounds like a cartoon. But these sounds do distract from conversation, which is supposed to be the focus of any meal, and draw too much attention to the diner and the food.

Smacking happens when you chew with your mouth open, even slightly. Quick fix? Close your mouth. Keep your lips completely together while there is any food yet to be swallowed. What exactly is slurping? It's the result of liquids, like soup or drinks, being inhaled rather than poured into your mouth. If you are using a spoon, the whole spoon bowl should go beyond your lips and your lips should clean it off on its way out. With a glass or cup, a small pour will put the liquid where you want it to be without the inhalation of more than you can handle in one sip. Chomping is common when our bites are too big for our mouths. This causes our lips to part to accommodate the chewing needed to swallow. Crunching doesn't necessarily come from eating crunchy foods (although chewing ice is always going to be loud); it comes from eating with your mouth open. If you want to quiet this, take small bites, allow the saliva in your mouth to start wetting the food and then chew. Oh, so much quieter now!

Watching Others Eat

"One of my pet peeves is a person who eats with mouth open, showing their partially masticated food to all."

—*Sandy Jolley*

It's not just the sound of our eating that is sometimes annoying; it's also having to watch it happen. Partially chewed food is gross—plain and simple. ***The Solution:*** There is an unspoken rule in power cities like Washington, D.C. and Los Angeles: Always eat in public as if the cameras were shooting the whole scene, and it will be printed on the front page of the *Washington Post* or *Los Angeles Times.* And for those of us who are annoyed by this behavior, politely tell the person eating that you don't like seeing his food in his mouth. There is no harm in making this known.

"[I become annoyed when] people who talk while their mouths are full of food and continue to talk even when the person tells them, 'Oh, I'm sorry, I caught you with a mouth full.'"

—*Charlotte Parris*

The proper thing to do if someone starts talking to you when you have just taken a bite (which is when most people talk to me at the table) is to look at him, perhaps nod, and hold up one finger using body language to say, "One minute. I will respond as soon as I can without being rude." If someone is talking to you with a mouth full of nasty, half-chewed food, discontinue eye contact with him and tell him that you'll be happy to speak with him once he's finished chewing. That should give him a good hint and will hopefully stop the annoying behavior.

> "I hate seeing people who have previously eaten food on the corners of their mouths after eating."
>
> —*Lance S. of Idaho*

It is embarrassing to have food all over your face, isn't it? But I don't know see why Lance is so disturbed—this is something that happens to most of us one time or another. ***The Solution:*** A kind thing to do would be to make eye contact with the offender, and point to and touch the place on your own face where the food is on his face. As human beings, we naturally mimic what others do and the offender will immediately check himself and take care to clear the food away. Be helpful to the person you are with and not only will the annoyance subside but you'll also make sure he isn't embarrassed after a whole meal with food on his face.

> "[I find myself getting annoyed by] people who can't seem to keep the food on their plate. It is either on the table or on them."
>
> —*Anonymous diners*

The Solution: In all honesty, it is best not to make any comments about the mess and just try to keep your annoyance in check. Concentrate on the conversation. However, if there is something that has dropped on the front of your companion's clothes and he seems unaware of it, it would be kind to make eye contact and point to yourself in the same place as the food is on him (or just excuse yourself and tell him that he has food on his shirt). This will allow him to clean it off, avoiding a stain later—and you won't have to be grossed out looking at sloppy dinner companions.

General Restaurant Annoyances

"[It's awful] finding a hair in my food after eating most of the course!"

—Grossed-out diner

I only received a small number of these types of complaints, but it is definitely on my personal annoyance list. If you find a hair in your food, before you start a tirade towards the restaurant manager, make certain that the hair didn't fall from your own head. If it is definitely a different color or texture than your own, you probably have a complaint. ***The Solution:*** Please be a gentle person. The hair is only in your food, not every other diner's. Either call the waiter to your table and quietly inform him what happened or get up from the table and tell him away from the other diners.

"[I get annoyed] when someone does not push in their chair after eating dinner."

—Several disgruntled diners

The Solution: If the offender is with my party, and I don't have to go fully around the table to push the chair in, I take it upon myself to follow through with this consideration for the others around us. If I would be in the way of the waitstaff or other diners by tending to this, I ignore it, assuming the waitstaff will take care of it as part of their job and let it go. Sometimes there are just bigger fish to fry.

"[I detest it when] people use toothpicks in a restaurant."

—Harry P. of Nebraska

In the United States, this is a common practice in some parts of the country. However, there is a proper way of handling a toothpick if you do use one in a restaurant. Cover your mouth with one hand while using the toothpick with the other. And please, if there is a difficult scrap caught, take it to the bathroom or outside where people at the table cannot watch the food dislodge from your teeth. And don't be shy of asking others to practice this common courtesy either.

> "[It's annoying] when I eat out and see men or boys wearing their hat at the table, even in the company of presumed ladies; it drives me nuts."
>
> —*Annoyed diner*

This is one of my personal annoyances when I eat out, but I am not alone in my concern for the lack of respect men of all ages have for the others who are dining with them. Hats are not part of the outfit—they are meant to cover your head when you go outdoors. Besides, they just look tacky at the dining table. However, it is also good to learn that you cannot always change the behavior of others. Though this certainly is annoying, it's not worth getting worked up over. Just remember that not everyone was raised knowing the proper rules of table etiquette and leave it at that. That being said, if I choose to fill out a comment card provided by the restaurant, I usually include one about not allowing men to wear hats inside the restaurant. I have seen this taken to heart by few restaurateurs during my life, so I don't get my hopes up.

Restaurant Waitstaff

> "It disturbs me when a waiter turns a wine glass or coffee cup over on its rim if the diner doesn't want to be served that beverage. A glass or cup should never show its bottom or "kiss" the tablecloth. It not only looks horrible on the table to the other diners but draws attention to the person who didn't want to be served that beverage."
>
> —*An anonymous crowd, including your humble author*

The Solution: Either wait until the waiter leaves and return the glass to its upright position, or when the waiter begins to turn over the glass, ask him to remove it from the table entirely. In both circumstances, he should get the hint and you'll have been proactive in quelling your annoyance level.

"My worst pet peeve is when the waiter holds your glass and has his/her hand on the rim then you have to drink from it and you see their finger marks all over the glass."

—*Kelly*

I don't blame Kelly for this complaint. ***The Solution:*** The best thing to do is to ask for another glass immediately, pointing out why you made that request so that the same waiter won't make the same mistake twice. You don't have to stand for drinking out of a dirty glass.

"[I find it incredibly annoying when at a restaurant] someone hovers over you looking at your food while you're eating."

—*Kitty W. of Indiana*

The (fun) Solution: Ask that person if he would like a taste. Most likely that will send him away pretty quickly and you'll be able to enjoy your meal, though you might receive glares from him.

Common Table Manners

A dining tutorial is apparently necessary for most adults who didn't learn the skills of successfully navigating through a meal from their parents. Most of the time, it isn't the parents' fault that the children don't know the proper procedures. The parents never learned either so they didn't know what they weren't teaching their kids. This book's intention is not a how-to guide for dining out, but there are more basic rules that, if practiced, will get you through a meal with more ease and less criticism.

Eleven Standard Rules for Good Table Etiquette:

1. Elbows off the table unless there are no plates at anyone's place and only glassware or coffee cups are left. Only one elbow should be on the table at a time and please don't lean on your chin.
2. Don't move your plate during the meal. Leave all moving to the waitstaff.
3. The 10 o'clock/4 o'clock position for resting your utensils is the proper position to indicate that you have finished the course and the waitstaff can remove your plate.
4. Soup is spooned away from you and the bottom of the spoon is wiped against the outside rim of the cup/bowl so no drips are brought to your mouth.
5. The contents of the soup spoon are eaten in one mouthful, not sipped or slurped resulting in noise. (Eating soup should be silent.)
6. Bread is broken into one bite-size piece at a time, buttered over the bread plate, knife returned to the bread plate, and eaten in one bite.
7. If food drops (without sauce) onto the table, discretely pick it off the table and put it back on your plate. Do not attempt to clear off bread crumbs, however. That will be done by the waiter when the course plate is removed.
8. Pass both the salt and pepper together even if only one is requested.
9. Pass all dishes to the right.
10. Your nose should not be within a foot of your plate. Food is brought up from your plate; your face is not dropped down to the plate.
11. Your tongue should never escape past the inside of the bottom teeth when taking a bite. (Thank you, Susan Houser for this tip.)

"My pet peeve is individuals who blow their nose at the dinner table. It would be polite if they would excuse themselves to the men's/ladies' room."

—*Patryce Collins and Susan Stein Lascko*

I will add my own personal annoyance to this one: people who blow their nose or cough into their napkin. Your cloth napkin, while gentle on your nose, is not a tissue and certainly not disposable. A real live human being has to pick up your snotty, germ-filled napkin and put it into the laundry after you leave the table. How disrespectful can one be to a stranger? The proper way to handle it is to sneeze into the crook of your arm. Turn your head and shoulder towards the left and away from the table (and the person sitting next to you) and sneeze (or cough) into your shirtsleeve. Or, if you carry your own handkerchief (once a common occurrence in polite society), by all means use it instead of your arm. If you have replaced the lovely handkerchief with a disposable tissue, that works too. Just put it into your pocket or purse as soon as you have finished using it so others won't see it. And feel free to teach those dining with you to do the same—it not only helps deter the spread of germs but it brings your annoyance level down to a proper level.

"My [annoyance is with] women who touch up their makeup, clean their teeth, and groom their hair at the dinner (table) get a clue: powder room."

—*Loretta Huggins*

Why would you want to show the world how much effort it takes to make you look as beautiful as you do? Putting on makeup and performing other grooming tasks are not sanitary at the table and they are meant to be private. Many women tell me that a quick lipstick fix isn't rude—nobody minds. According to proper etiquette, the rule of private primping is broken even with the quick fix. But beyond the rules, though many people will tell you they don't mind if another diner at the table does the lipstick fix, if you press them on the issue,

I have found that they will admit that it makes them uncomfortable because while the woman is primping, they don't know what to do with themselves. Should they continue the conversation with her or look the other way? **The Solution:** If you are a woman and your fellow diner is also a woman, as soon as you see her bring out her compact, ask if she would like to join you in a trip to the ladies' room. If you are a gentleman, look away and try not to engage her while she is primping. At a different time, you might mention how it makes you uncomfortable when she adjusts her makeup at the table. And be sure to add that she doesn't need it—she's beautiful just the way she is. "People talking on cell phones while eating out—the sounds of eating that the listener on the other end must endure are disrespectful and rude."

—C. Markham from Austin, Texas

This is a great point. You already know how annoying hearing and watching others talk on cell phones is in a restaurant, but the crunching and chewing indicates to the person on the other end that conversation with him is not as important as having his meal. **The Solution:** Ask your friend to put the phone away while you are eating with him. That will not only solve your annoyance with his rude behavior but will also spare the person on the other end of the call from hearing loud chomping noses in his ear.

"Slurping soup [is extremely annoying]."

—Complaint from many diners

Slurping soup is so common that it is has become the cliche of bad table manners. When eating soup, we know you spoon it away from yourself so that you are less likely to splatter it on your clothes. When you bring the spoon to your mouth, everything on the spoon should go into your mouth in one swoop and a clean spoon should emerge. **The Solution:** Unless you are eating at a Japanese restaurant (where it is the custom to slurp soup and noodles), a gentle reminder to your dining companion (or a good set of earplugs if eating out alone) should solve this dilemma.

"[It ruins my meal when] people burp and make other bodily sounds while I am eating."

—*Kenny from New York City*

Here's the truth of the matter: It would be even ruder to say anything to the offender which would cause embarrassment and perhaps shame. If the person says, "Excuse me," smile and say, "You're excused" and then drop it. If no excuse is made, the best reaction is to either approach him in private about the situation or accept it as that person's personality, but keep it in mind if you plan a fancy meal with others whom you are trying to impress. You know what they say about the company you keep.

Using Utensils (or a Lack Thereof)

"It baffles me how many people do not know how to use a fork and knife properly. Then they also fail to put the knife and fork together on the plate when finished."

—*Fay*

I too wish we didn't all have to watch others use their knife and fork like a saw and pitchfork or observe people holding these utensils like pipe cleaners. Most of us start using our utensils around the age of four. At that point it is safe to say that parents' main concern isn't how their children are holding their utensils but their success in getting food from the plate to the child's mouth. I spend a good portion of time in the dining tutorials I facilitate, reteaching adults how to hold their knife, fork, and spoon. ***The Solution:*** Be your own etiquette teacher and give your friend a lesson in proper utensil usage. But do this in a private location, such as your own kitchen. If you think this would embarrass your friend too much, arrange for an outsider to do the teaching for both of you. If you are annoyed with the way strangers use their utensils, just sit back and be happy that you, at least, don't look like a fool when cutting your food.

An aside: On multiple lists of savvy diners is the frustration of having to see other diners "oaring" their utensils. This is when the knife and/or fork are laid against the plate with the handle on the table and the blade or tines leaning against the edge of the plate. The etiquette rule is that once you pick up a utensil from the table, it never touches the table again. Lay your knife and fork, tines down, across the plate in an inverted V if you are eating with both hands continental style. If you are eating American or zigzag style, the knife is laid across the edge of the plate on the right side with the cutting edge facing the center of the plate while you are not using it. The fork is laid tines up in the 4 o'clock position while you rest or take a drink. When you are finished with the course, all utensils, used or not, are placed on the plate in the 4 o'clock position. If you are eating continental style, the tines of the fork are face down. If you ate American style, the tines are up.

"It's annoying to watch people eat with their fingers."

—*Many, many diners*

Eating with your hands (unless appropriate) is a symptom of both not knowing proper table manners and also the casualness that has pervaded our sensibilities when we go out. We no longer consider eating outside our homes as being special, requiring we put on our best behavior. We have adopted a "take me or leave me" attitude toward how others see our manners. ***The Solution:*** The only influence you can have when someone is eating something with his fingers that clearly should be eaten with a fork is to model the appropriate way to eat. If he doesn't get the hint, maybe he won't be the first person you ask to join you for the next meal out.

"People scraping their teeth on utensils when eating [is annoying]!"

—*Anonymous group of people*

I agree that people using their teeth to get the last little bit of food in their mouths look like they are starving. ***The Solution:*** Sometimes just grimacing while you watch will stop the offensive behavior.

> "While eating, scraping a dinner plate with your fork until it squeaks [is an annoying habit]."
>
> —*Sensitive eaters*

The Solution: A quiet comment to the person whose fork is doing the scraping such as, "I'm sorry, but that really bothers me" will bring his attention to a bad habit of which I am sure he is unaware and more than willing to work on.

Shelly Miller shared that on a recent date, her boyfriend caused a situation that lands on her list of annoying dinner behavior. They were eating at a fancy restaurant and the meal was filet mignon, mashed potatoes, and green beans. It was a very nice meal—until the mashed potatoes ended up on her silk blouse. Her boyfriend often uses his knife as a pointer during conversation and on this particular evening, a glob of mashed potatoes was stuck on the edge of the blade. When he shook his "pointer" at her to emphasize an opinion, the potatoes flew off and landed smack in the middle of her chest. The cause and effect speaks for itself regarding the proper use of a knife. So if you see someone using his utensils as an extension of his limbs, make sure you are out of harm's way (or the trajectory of any flying food particles)—and remind him to leave his utensils on his plate while he is talking.

Food Conversations

> "[I easily get annoyed] when I'm eating, and people are talking about how they don't like what I'm eating."
>
> —*Connie G. from Washington, D.C.*

Conversation at the table while eating is generally not something to complain about unless you feel as though you're being attacked for your food preferences. Good manners dictate that we keep our opinions about others' choices of food to ourselves, particularly while they are enjoying it. *The Solution:* We should never be put into the position of having to defend our food but if this annoys you, tell the person that you enjoy your meal and appreciate that it isn't to his taste. Be assertive and brush it off.

> "It's frustrating when someone says to me, 'You're eating that?'"
>
> —*One self-conscious diner*

This can leave you with an unsettled feeling about what you have ordered and, until that comment, thought was quite tasty. *The Solution:* The best answer to that kind of statement is, "Oh yes! It is terrific! Would you like to try it?" My guess is that will be the end of discussion about your choice.

Miscellaneous Annoyances When Eating with Others

> "People eating a huge amount in one bite [is a problem for me]."
>
> —*Anonymous*

One woman thinks this is a way for her friend to purposefully stop a conversation when it turns to something she doesn't want to discuss. Whether this is true or not, many people think that watching someone fill his mouth full—to the point of filling one's cheeks—in just one bite is one of the most undesirable dining behaviors. Not only does this make the eater look gluttonous but it puts you in the position of having to hold up your side of the conversation for a much longer stretch than expected. But, it could be a good time to make a point that the other diner ignored in the past, because he cannot speak up at the moment. *The Solution:* Just be thankful that you don't have to resort to stuffing your cheeks to get out of a conversation, and move on.

"People who suck their fingers while eating drive me crazy!"
                                    —*Martin W. from New Orleans, LA*

Not only do these people inevitably put their fingers back into their food, but now they have saliva on them. Napkins were invented for a purpose. The best you can do, however, is model proper use of the napkin and hope they catch on.

"People who cut up everything on their plate as soon as it is laid in front of them [annoy me]."
                                    —*Paul O. from Milwaukee, WI*

These people do look like they are cutting up their meal for a child. The etiquette rule is that you cut one piece at a time then put it into your mouth. Some experts will allow up to three pieces at a time. But please, no more than three or we will be looking for the three-year-old who has joined us at the table. Now that you know the proper etiquette for this annoyance, be confident in passing it along to those who cut their steak into little nubbins.

"People touching food in public and not eating it [is so annoying]."
                                    —*Anonymous*

Take this example: As the bread rolls are passed around the table (of course they are passed to the right as etiquette dictates), many diners share that when someone picks up the various rolls before deciding to commit to eating just one and putting it on his plate, he decides at that point that bread with dinner will have to wait for another evening. They do not know for sure if the uncouth bread chooser has washed his hands prior to touching the communal bread. I suggest that if someone touches a piece of something with his hands and leaves it on the service plate for an unsuspecting someone to choose later, I pick it up with my fork or spoon and put it to the side on a different plate so germs won't be spread. I do this for both my benefit (I know now what not to choose for myself and therefore do not need to become annoyed) but also for the benefit of the other diners. It doesn't matter if the person who did the touching notices or not—all that matters is that you'll be sure to pick a roll with no germs.

"When my friend and I eat out, if I order something she thinks looks good, she just reaches over and starts eating off my plate."

—*Bob Green from Florida*

The Solution: Try telling her that, though you would be happy to share a little by putting it on her bread plate, you would appreciate it if you could have your meal to yourself. If she gets offended, ask her if she would like to switch meals. She will probably say no. Sometime, when you are away from a restaurant, it would be helpful to her if you shared your dislike of having her help herself off your plate. She may have never been told it is annoying before.

The Random, the Strange, and the Downright Silly Annoyances:

Throughout my research, I sometimes came across unusual, odd, or irrational annoyances. Here are my favorite complaints from people regarding eating with others.

1. "People who breathe through their nose while eating" was a common annoyance for many people. I have to admit, this was a new one for me. I personally cannot get annoyed with people for breathing. Even if the breathing is labored or loud, there are just some behaviors you must allow others to engage in. Breathing is at the top of my list of "can't get annoyed with others for doing."

2. "I hate the sound of someone eating a banana!" Well, I must always be around people who eat bananas quietly and with dignity because I'm not sure how eating a banana could be

annoying. I do know of a few chimps in the National Zoo who could use an etiquette lesson on peeling and using a trash can for the leftovers.

3. Eating pizza with a knife and fork bothers many people who were never taught that the original and proper term for "pizza" is "pizza pie." There are many people who don't like to eat with their fingers for sanitary or tactile reasons. For them, a knife and fork works best. To judge someone harshly because he eats a slice of anything on bread (sandwiches included) with utensils instead of his fingers is not taking into consideration that the neat diner may be onto something.

4. "People who hold their food in their hands the entire time they are eating without putting it down once" (a sandwich, for example). Well, they certainly would have a hard time taking a drink of water, I suppose.

5. "My grandmother eating dinner at 6:00" is annoying to Pearl V. of Ft. Myers, Florida. When you get older, Pearl, you naturally get hungry a little earlier than you did in your teens or twenties. If you have children, you also tend to change your dinner time to accommodate feeding them. Getting upset about when someone else eats is unfair, in my opinion.

6. "I hate people who take their teeth out, right at the table, when they get through eating!" This gem was received from Elijah Billings in Miami, Florida, and I'll tell you, I don't plan on eating where he eats because I concur that this would be pretty distracting and unsanitary.

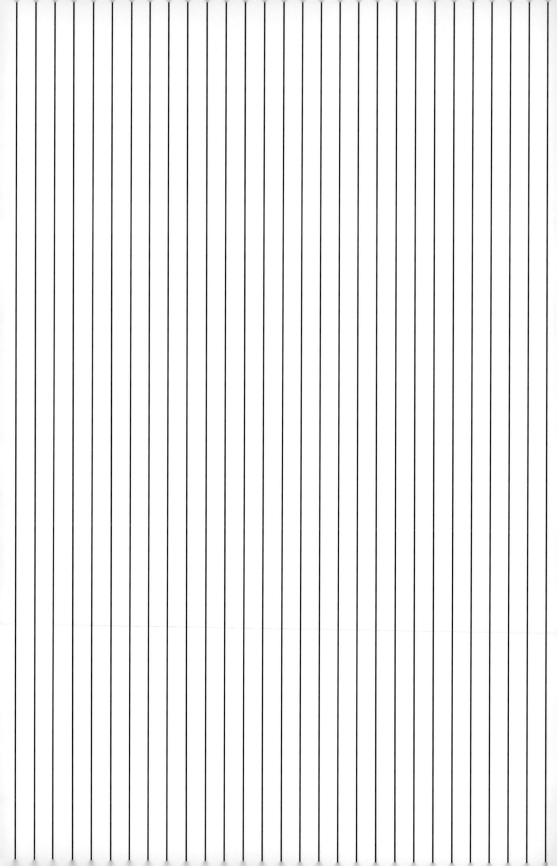

CHAPTER 3

WORKING WITH OTHERS

If we work outside of our homes, we spend the majority of our days in an office, thinking about work, doing work, trying to get out of doing work, and dealing with our coworkers and clients. That is a lot of interpersonal communication. Whenever people are put together for a common purpose but don't really know each other (and find it hard to see eye-to-eye on many common issues) irritations are bound to surface. Finding annoyances in the workplace is an extremely common occurrence. Because most of us work outside of our homes and have to deal with these frustrations on a daily basis, it is important to know how to react in the face of bad office behavior.

Is rudeness in the workplace on the rise? Do you think it is the managers' responsibility to create a more considerate culture among the office staff? Have you ever not reported rudeness to your manager or supervisor because you were worried about being accused of being too sensitive?

> According to an article in the *Wall Street Journal* (online, accessed on January 19, 2006) titled "Rise in Office Rudeness Weighs on Productivity and Retention":
>
> ♦ E-mail and phone communication is being used more than face- to-face communication.
> ♦ Fifty percent of 3,000 people polled say they lost work time worrying about an incident in the workplace. Fifty percent contemplated changing jobs to avoid a recurrence.
> ♦ One in eight said they left a company because of a rude incident.

Before we continue with how to deal with common annoyances in the office, I think it's important to touch on the subject of general rudeness. In response to our current "'F-Word' Culture," a report on TheLadders.co.uk looked at how seriously senior managers viewed manners and office etiquette. Office etiquette was important to ninety-seven percent of respondents, and fifty-seven percent said they would fire an employee for bad manners. Official warnings for etiquette offenses were given by seventy-six percent for infractions such as a messy desk, teeth flossing, nose picking, bad breath, or wearing athletic shoes. In order to stave off these bad behaviors and also to keep ourselves from becoming annoyed with fellow employees, we need to be aware of our own actions, model acceptable behavior, and not be afraid to pull a coworker aside and let him know that his behavior is unprofessional and creates an uncomfortable work environment.

Bosses

When it comes to our bosses, we seem to be exceptionally critical, and our annoyance level skyrockets. We are especially sensitive to those who wield power over us (perceived or true) and we are extra defensive

---

The Top Ten Office Etiquette Offenses Deemed Unacceptable by Senior Managers

1. Bad hygiene—smelly breath, dirty clothes, etc.
2. Bad language
3. Bad personal habits—flossing teeth with a paperclip, picking one's nose, etc.
4. Wastefulness
5. Not offering to share chores
6. Eating smelly food in the office
7. Eating someone else's food out of the fridge/from his desk
8. Messy desk/office area and littering
9. Loud talking
10. BlackBerry in meetings

---

about being put down. However, it is imperative that we learn how to react effectively to our bosses' annoying behavior because, after all, they are the ones in charge—and the ones who have the hiring (and firing) power.

> "It's annoying to work for a boss who doesn't know as much as I do about what I am doing."
>
> —*A common complaint among office workers*

Just a heads-up: The common wisdom in business is to surround yourself with people who know more than you do about a job's details and use your managerial talents to manage. Unfortunately, the reality is that many organizations promote great and knowledgeable workers into the position of "boss" and that person doesn't know the first thing about being a manager, and because his job is no longer a day-to-day practice of the skills which got him the promotion, he loses touch with the details. ***The Solution:*** Take pride in the fact that you actually have an understanding of the task you've been hired to accomplish—see it as a sign of respect and trust on the part of your employer and don't let it get on your nerves.

> ## "It's so frustrating having a boss with inadequate spelling and writing skills."
> —*Disgruntled memo-reading employees*

I received hundreds of complaints about having to decipher e-mails from a boss who can't express him- or herself clearly. These bosses may not even realize what a strong negative impression their bad writing gives. ***The Solution:*** I suggest that you have a face-to-face meeting with your boss, bringing to his attention his spelling mistakes. Remember that the way you approach this problem is most important and could even result in a better position for you. Say something like, "Mr. Boss, I know your reputation is as important to you as it is to all of us. I don't know whether you are aware of this or not, but your spelling in your e-mails distracts from the importance of your words and that could be hurting you. I just thought you would want to know." I don't know the immediate feedback you might receive, but I guarantee your boss will look more carefully at any e-mails he sends in the future. It is one thing to become annoyed by each misspelled word but it is so much more proactive and productive for you if you can be a resource for behavior modification.

> ## "Bosses who abuse their power, exert undue authority over their employees, and genuinely don't appreciate those who work on their team are not only annoying but hurtful."
> —*Underappreciated employees*

It's sad but true—these types of supervisors are to be pitied rather than attacked. There are bosses who give the impression that they think they are always right. From my experience, these people are the ones who have the greatest inferiority complexes and compensate by trying to put their subordinates down by bullying them in the workplace. Bad bosses who try to intimidate their employees are either trying to look tough and managerial to their own boss or have exceptionally poor interpersonal skills. What these people don't realize is that bullying eventually backfires, and they will suffer at some point in their career for the way they treat their team. My suggestion is that if you are bullied at work and find this incredibly frustrating, you need to not only stand up for yourself but also try to help rather than react negatively. It has been my experience that if you approach a bully with an abundance of niceness rather than contempt, you will catch that aggressive person off guard and gain power over the situation. Then, you can work together to build a better working relationship—one that you can stand and one that your boss can effectively manage.

"My boss always brings her personal problems to work. It's very annoying."

—*Anonymous*

To be fair, we all have personal problems that we cannot help but take to the office on occasion. Your boss is no exception. ***The Solution:*** Show some empathy for the pressure your boss may be under, most of which you are not even aware, and display willingness to make life a little easier for him. This could make it much more pleasant for you and your coworkers (and will give your boss some needed support at work). I can just hear you thinking "Why should I be nice to that jerk?" Well, as Dr. Phil McGraw often asks: "How is it working for you the other way?" It may be worth a try—especially if it allays your annoyance for the time being.

"I work as an administrative assistant, and I hate it when people ask if I can 'have' or 'get' my boss to call them. I wish I had that power!! Unfortunately, I can only ask them to call."

—*Lisa S. from New York City*

Being asked to accomplish something you have no power to accomplish is certainly annoying but you should try to look at it this way: The person asking assumes you do have power and that can't be all that bad. Lisa S. also cited annoyance "when [her] boss messes something up but blames it on [her]" or when "[her] boss doesn't tell the truth." We are particularly sensitive when someone blames a mishap on us when that person is the one who clearly made the mistake. It's frustrating when someone accuses us of a lack of ability or integrity for not confessing the problem (which we ultimately did not create). What we have in this situation is a need for conversation in private with our boss. Explain what you heard and demand that you get the truth. If you can convince your boss how much more respect he will receive from the others in the office by admitting to mistakes (taking ownership away from you), you will have done your boss and coworkers a great favor, and you won't have to deal with this annoyance any longer.

> "It's annoying that bosses seem to fart much more than most other people."
>
> —*Anonymous employees around the country*

It seems likely, from the enormity of responses on this subject, that people believe bosses fart more than any other person. But let's take this one step further: Maybe employees are more aware of their boss's indiscretion with passing gas because they are looking for something negative to say about the person in charge. It is a medical fact that human beings pass gas an average of nineteen times a day. The vast majority of the time, only the perpetrator would know of it because of the location or general sound level in the room. We also don't notice it in most people because we have been around it since infancy. However, when our boss passes gas, it is one more thing we judge him for that can be a check in the negative column. It also could be more noticeable if he doesn't excuse himself if he realizes it was audible. When we like someone, we are more likely to give that person the benefit of the doubt in everything he does. We allow the halo effect to take hold if the other person has shown us respect and consideration. If the other person is our boss, who has been on our case or who has embarrassed us in some way, our knee-jerk reaction to something like this is to criticize and ridicule it. ***The Solution:*** Reevaluate why this normal bodily function would annoy you so much and if you find the annoyance to be elsewhere, deal with that larger problem—and leave the flatulence out of it.

Cubicles

The Twenty Most Common Issues with Cubicle Mates

1. Speakerphones
2. Music on hold that plays out loud because the speakerphone is on
3. Personal phone calls
4. Cubicle popularity (three-plus people in one cubicle at a time)
5. Dead plants and flowers
6. Jumping up to look over the wall to make eye contact (the gopher syndrome)
7. Decor that is too unprofessional, too personal, or involves stuffed animals
8. Eating in the cubicle and not cleaning up after yourself
9. Not using headsets when listening to music or podcasts
10. Bodily noises
11. Too much perfume/cologne
12. Loud jewelry banging on the desk
13. Yawning loudly
14. Talking to oneself/self-congratulations out loud
15. Being interrupted by someone who walks into the cubicle without knocking
16. Never having any privacy
17. Using nail clippers
18. People who use speakerphones in the office when calling someone one cube away
19. People who sing and whistle to music in the cubicle thinking others want to hear it
20. Shouting over cubicle walls

In modern offices all over the world cubicles are here to stay. Cubicles are often justified as space-saving measures or as giving the impression of transparency in the workplace. I have never met a cubicle-dweller who preferred it to an office with a door, but knowing how to handle the specific challenges cubicle life presents (as well as how to stave off our common annoyances with cubicle mates) can be the difference between a good and bad day, every day of your working life.

Solutions for Irksome Cubicle Behaviors

1. Suggest to your speakerphone-loving cohort that instead of using the speakerphone at his cubicle desk, find an empty conference room to hold that specific conversation.
2. Visit the cubicle from which the noise is emitting and ask the occupant to remove the speakerphone so you can concentrate. There is no shame in trying to get your work done.
3. Politely ask your cubicle mate to take his personal calls outside of the office (preferably on his cell phone in another part of the building or room). Emphasize that people generally don't want to know who is calling him and that you feel as though you are eavesdropping on his private conversation, which makes you uncomfortable.
4. Remember that people are allowed to have fun at work from time to time, and socializing with your coworkers can help foster a better office environment. If this is something that occurs on a daily basis and it interferes with your concentration, speak to the cubicle's owner or your manager and express your exasperation with the situation. Be open to suggestions and try to come to some reasonable mutual agreement.
5. Be a good neighbor and ask if you can water your coworker's plants if their imminent death is bothering you. Be proactive!
6. If you notice someone doing this to you, don't make eye contact when he becomes a cubicle "gopher": Wait to speak with him until he approaches you at normal eye level.

7. If there isn't a company policy against bringing in personal effects to decorate a cubicle then there is little you can do but avoid going into the one with stuffed animals all over the desk.

8. Bugs! Maybe a friendly memo or e-mail reminder that you don't want bugs infesting the office would help deter messes.

9. As with the speakerphone blaring "hold" music, just approach the guilty employee and ask that he use headphones so you can work more effectively.

10. As I've said before—it's a part of life.

11. Politely ask the person to refrain from using so much perfume/cologne as you find yourself getting congested due to the odor. Tell him it's a lovely smell but a little goes a long way. If you are truly allergic to the cologne, don't allow the situation to fester. Share your health concern with the spritzer as soon as you notice it.

12. Though this certainly can be annoying, it is hard to tell someone what he can and cannot wear, especially if it's not stated in the company handbook. Remember that you are also making noises in your cubicle that others can hear and let this annoyance go.

13. Some people just do this for attention and others just don't recognize how loud their "yawn" is. This probably doesn't happen nonstop all day, so just grin and bear it—and remember your annoyance the next time you need to yawn.

14. Again, it's hard to control other people's inappropriate behavior. If you share a cubicle wall with someone like this, and these pep talks occur frequently, perhaps investing in a pair of earplugs would stifle the noise (and the frustration).

15. You have every right to request that people knock and say, "excuse me" before entering your work space. Make that point clear the first time you are interrupted and it probably won't happen again. I have even seen signs on the outside of cubicles that inform the guest of proper entrance etiquette. "Please knock!" is easy to understand.

16. Stagger your lunch times with cubicle mates so that everyone has at least thirty minutes of private time during the day.

17. Yes, this is gross. If you feel bold enough, tell the person clipping that you would rather he did that in the bathroom. If you aren't so bold, maybe this would be a good time for you to take a bathroom break and remove yourself from the annoyance.

18. Be assertive and tell your coworkers that this is frustrating you and · that you'd prefer if he would just e-mail or go talk to the person next door. Some people prefer phone conversations to face-to-face meetings and so you need to be mindful of this. But you don't need to deal with the speakerphone.

19. Again, this is a case-by-case incident. If it really bothers you but you don't want to approach the person, get some earplugs. If you feel comfortable pulling the coworker aside and expressing your frustration, I'm sure you can work something out. Remember that sometimes people don't know that they are speaking or singing aloud.

20. Well, you are in an office and people will inevitably do this. You can be annoyed but is it really worth stressing out about?

Messy Office Environments

"Sloppy offices and messy desks make me feel less comfortable in the office or [when] working with the person who is responsible for the mess. It also grates on my nerves."

—Anonymous

The office is a collection of personalities and habits. It is a working environment in which some people need a clean, orderly space to do their best work and others are perfectly comfortable working in a sloppy mess. It's true that we tend to make judgments about our coworkers and their ability to a good job on tasks and projects based on how they dress, how they interact with others, and how their offices look. ***The Solution:*** If this is an office-wide problem, bring it up with your boss or supervisor and have a plan of action for "cleaning the office." If this relates only to one of your coworkers, politely address him about the issue and see if you can offer some suggestions about cleaning.

Food at Work

"It's annoying when coworkers take only half of something in a communal food situation, as if someone else would want the other half after it looks tainted."

—*Frustrated coworkers*

It is common for people to act the same way they do at home in the office. Most families accept the "cut it in half because I don't want the whole thing" act with food at home. It is called sharing in most eyes. But we don't usually share with strangers and that is where the annoyance comes from. ***The Solution:*** Don't take just a little of something. Take the whole item and leave what you don't want on your plate. I know that is wasteful. You can ask someone else if he would share the donut with you before you dig into it and then each get half. That would take care of the calorie count and the wastefulness. If there is no one else around just assume no one wants to share with you.

"I'm annoyed when fellow workers don't pick up their own lunch dishes and clean them off in the sink."

—*Peter M. from St. Thomas, U.S. Virgin Islands*

This is certainly an annoying issue because not only can bugs accept the invitation implied by the food left on the counter and plates, but also this doesn't leave a good impression on any client who might enter the kitchen and see what slobs the workers are. ***The Solution:*** Post a notice above the sink imploring the other employees to clean up their dishes and silverware. Your mom most likely taught you to clean up after yourself—now it's your turn to "mother" others and teach them to respect the work space.

Office Meetings

Key Complaints

"Meetings that are meaningless [annoy me]."

"Meetings that just waste time [are very frustrating]."

"Sitting in a meeting when I could actually be doing something constructive [is so annoying]."

These are typical grievances in the business world. Most business-people believe that a meeting is getting everyone together to talk about what is happening and then magically something is accomplished that furthers the success of the company. That can unfortunately be far from the truth. Meetings are gatherings but they must have a designated purpose and agenda or they are just a waste of everyone's time. The purpose of the meeting needs to be established at the time of invitation and a plan sent out to all participants at least three hours prior to the meeting.

The complaints go further, addressing lateness to the meeting; participants leaving early without warning; messy eating at the conference table; using PDAs to text message and read e-mails while the participants are talking; hearing cell phones go off, especially with silly or distracting ringtones; and rooms that are too hot, too cold, or too noisy. **The Solution:** Be proactive in making your experience at the meeting as productive as possible. Go into the meeting with an open mind, knowing that others will most likely display bad behavior throughout. Model the good behavior you want to see in the meeting environment, and if you are having trouble concentrating due to excessive noise or environmental issues, raise your hand, excuse the interruption, and address these grievances. Chances are, you are not the only one stewing at this point. Know too that if you are the one leading the meeting, you are able to set the rules. You can request the quieting of all cell phones and PDAs. You can ask another employee if you don't know the procedure to make certain the temperature and noise level of the room are conducive to work.

Office Parties

> "Other coworkers get out of hand at office parties, ruining them for everyone else."
>
> —*Anonymous office workers*

Holiday celebrations or retirement parties are business-related functions. This means you are still at work when you attend them. Drinking too much, talking too much about inappropriate subjects (the raise you want, the error-filled project your office mate is dealing with, how cute he or she thinks the boss is) are all going to contribute to the success or lack of success of the event. ***The Solution:*** Keep in mind some key points that apply to office or company celebrations and don't be afraid to tell others about these rules of proper office party conduct:

1. Wear office clothes or modest party clothes—nothing shoulderless, low cut, or abbreviated. Heels should be the height you would normally wear to the office.
2. Don't drink more than one alcoholic drink if you imbibe.
3. Don't leave before the boss or most senior person leaves.
4. Don't come late.
5. Circulate. Meet people you don't know.
6. Don't skip it unless you have a really good excuse and you tell your boss ahead of time that you won't be there. He should not be looking for you.
7. Don't talk about other people unfavorably.
8. Don't gossip.
9. Don't bring guests who have not been specifically invited as a plus one.

Don't use the party as an excuse to flirt with the cute man or woman in the other department unless you are absolutely sure they are available and interested. And if you are feeling uncomfortable with someone at the office party, feel confident enough to tell that person the next day that you didn't appreciate his behavior (or bring it up to a supervisor).

Interviews (Part 1 – The Interviewer)

Key Complaints

(These complaints were given by hotel manager Andrew W., but they reflect many annoyances interviewers face)

1. The interviewee is constantly looking at his watch (making it seems as though the interview is boring).

2. The interviewee says that he has absolutely no faults.

3. The interviewee shows up unprepared and underdressed for the interview.

4. The interviewee does not put his best foot forward during the interview.

The Solution: You, as the interviewer, have the power to hire someone or not. We know you quickly make your decision as you talk with someone. If you are the one being interviewed in the future, take heed of what is being shared here:

Angela S., who works in restaurant corporate management, told me this about interviewing people: "An interview is a time for a candidate interested in a position to prove they have the qualifications necessary to perform well in the open position. The candidate should use the interview as an opportunity to 'sell' him- or herself to the company. My biggest pet peeve while interviewing a candidate is a candidate's excessive lack of knowledge regarding the company and position responsibilities. Candidates should perform initial research on the company and position details before they enter an interview. Many interviewers ask questions about the company to determine the candidate's interest level and commitment to working for the company. It is always important to be over prepared for an interview than to be under prepared."

Did you know that studies among human resources employees have found that the number one reason a candidate is not offered a job after being taken for a lunch interview is because the interviewee salted the food before tasting it? The common sense behind this decision is that the employee who will act without assessing the situation cannot be trusted to do the right thing for the company. So, as an interviewer who is dealing with annoying situations and job candidates on a regular basis, just stick true to your company's hiring policy (and your own gut) and wait until you find the best person possible for the job.

Interviews
(Part 2–The Interviewee)

"I disdain interviews because you research the company, you go to the interview, you put your best effort forward, you write a thank you note, and you never hear from the company again. It is not right!"

—*Anne Johnson from Dallas, TX*

This is always a very annoying part of job searches, but you don't have to let it get the best of you. ***The Solution:*** If you've interviewed for a company, you deserve to hear that you a) weren't chosen for the position and b) why you were not chosen. So if it's been some time since you heard from a job you interviewed for, call the company and ask to speak with the person who conducted your interview. Tell him that you are still wondering if the position is available and if he says no, be strong and ask why you weren't notified and why you did not get the position. You deserve to get at least a simple answer.

Miscellaneous Office Annoyances

"The Staple Artist is someone in your office who is too lazy to take out the old staples and just adds more staples to the paperwork."

—*Daniella*

The Solution: When I encountered this person in an office I used to work in, I gave her a staple remover with a note attached that said that I knew she must not have one of these because all of her paperwork has multiple staples. I noticed the clean documents immediately.

"[I'm annoyed] when I come back to the office from sick leave and someone asks how I am feeling. I reply, 'Better, thanks' and they respond, 'It looks like you've been sick!' What can you say to that?"

—*Nina W. of Long Island, New York*

The Solution: Sure, you probably feel a bit combative and want to say something like, "You look pretty bad yourself." But . . . a better response would definitely be, "Thank you for your concern, but I feel much better and I am glad to be back."

"I see young women in my office coming in dressed as if they are scouting for a man or ready for the clubs. Their hair is wild, their cleavage is prominent, their heels too high and skirts too short. It actually makes the men in the office uncomfortable because they don't want to be accused of staring or glaring or fawning all over them."

—*J.J. from San Francisco*

This is a very common occurrence especially in bigger cities and with young employees who have never been taught the appropriate image that the company expects from them. *The Solution:* It is time for the boss to say something. If you are not the boss, express your concern to your manager. If you are the boss, don't just let it annoy you—assert your superior role and have a talk with the inappropriately dressed woman. I know that some male bosses may feel awkward saying something to these young women. If this is the case, get human resources or a senior woman in the office involved who can explain the corporate culture, policy, and expectations to the younger women workers.

"Gossip in the workplace is often out of control. In an office with rows of cubicles a person who has a conflict with a coworker decides to discuss it in the open environment for everyone else to hear. A person should always take up confrontational conversation in the privacy of an office or away from communal areas."

—Heather

Gossip is an office faux pas that can get offenders into a lot of trouble. If you keep in mind that anything you personally didn't witness or experience is actually gossip, you will realize that spreading information about others in a closed environment can produce devastating results. Your accusations or observations are probably wrong, and the alleged perpetrator will suffer unfairly. Have you ever been the target of gossip? How did that affect you? Did you have to work to get your positive reputation back? Was the gossip true? Many people have a good time talking about others, but are really talking about themselves in disguise. "Maybe if I shed negative attention on her, what I did won't look so bad" is sometimes the motivation. ***The Solution:*** If you are annoyed by office gossip, ask the gossipers to refrain from speaking about coworkers in front of other office staff. Tell them that they should save that for outside of the office.

"It bothers me to see people with name tags on the left side of their chest. If I try to read their name, I have to direct my line of vision across their body and it feels and looks awkward. The proper placement for the name tag is on the right shoulder— the direct line of vision when two people shake hands is first the eyes and then it drops to the right shoulder. It only makes sense to put your name where it is easily and discreetly seen and read."

—*Many disgruntled employees*

I suggest that if you find this an annoying practice, then be sure to model the appropriate place to wear a name tag on your own body. A gentle remark such as, "I'm sorry, what is your name? I couldn't see your name tag" might be just enough of a hint to get people to change.

"My pet peeve about name tags is the lanyards that many conventions have you wear so the name badge is sitting in the center of your chest. All day long men are staring at my chest in an effort to see my name. It makes me feel really uncomfortable."

—*Woman at an engineering conference*

This is one of my complaints too. It may be rebellious, but I refuse to wear the lanyard. I understand that they are used so that a person's clothing isn't pierced with a pin but I would rather clip or pin my name badge on my right shoulder so that others can see it than have them staring at the middle of my chest all day. If you can't refuse to wear the lanyard, then I suggest trying to shorten the string by wrapping it twice around your neck. Then at least the name tag part won't be hanging in the center of your chest but up higher like a necklace.

"I'm annoyed when women bring their personal shopping to the office and show it off to their friends."

—*Discerning employees*

I agree that showing off a new CD shouldn't be a problem, but it gets embarrassing when the items are lingerie and such. ***The Solution:*** Take the personal shopper aside and ask her (politely) if she would refrain from bringing in her very personal purchases to display around the office. Explain that you and others feel uncomfortable seeing her undergarments and she will, most likely, feel somewhat embarrassed that others noticed her display.

"It's frustrating being 'nickeled and dimed' at the office for someone's charity or for a gift that everyone is chipping in for."

—*Anonymous coworkers*

Asking for money, in any situation, can cause a great deal of anxiety. Salaries are tight, budgets are tight, and we don't have the inclination to give up our lunch money to contribute to something we hadn't previously wanted to donate to. ***The Solution:*** If you are asked to give money to some charity or gift, and you don't wish to participate for whatever reason, you have the power to say no. But say it nicely. "I hope you get enough for what you intend to buy but I can't participate at this time. I will be happy to sign the card" should be sufficient response. No explanation is necessary, and actually, it would be better if you didn't offer one.

"People who call the office one minute after closing time and expect service are very annoying and rude."

—*Common service industry complaint*

For some reason the public doesn't respect that workers who are now free to leave and attend to their private lives might actually want to do that instead of dropping their plans and waiting on a late customer. ***The Solution:*** If you are the employee who has been asked to stay because your best customer has come in a minute or two after closing, and you value the customer's business, it is certainly your responsibility to stay and help. But also feel free to inform the customer that the store is closed and that you'd like to help find anything needed as efficiently as possible. This should, hopefully, give your customer the hint and get you out of the door as soon as possible.

"I find it extremely annoying when an employee decides to call in absent without sufficient cause or notice.

Furthermore, it is worse when that employee throws a bombshell by announcing that he/she is quitting the job with immediate effect without bothering to arrange for a replacement or relief."

—*Indru Mansukhani*

This is a frustration for businesses everywhere and a situation that hurts other employees as well as the management. Though we should do what is right for ourselves, to maintain our business reputation we need to think about how others will be affected and minimize the damage caused by calling in sick or quitting. ***The Solution:*** If you are annoyed by someone who unexpectedly quits (and you are in a position of authority to question the action), you should feel free to bring up this concern to the employee and say that you would have appreciated more notice. If, on the other hand, you are annoyed with someone for calling in sick without proper notice, this might be a situation that just can't be helped. Sometimes people wake up and are just too ill to go to work—try to empathize with them and not take this too much to heart. Who knows? Someday *you* might be in need of a little consideration.

A Side Note: The Office "Jerk"

In offices all over the world, many of the same concerns and annoyances abound. Many of these frustrations are fairly easy to resolve in a calm and professional manner. But what happens to a company (and its employees) when the workplace is invaded by jerks? How can we deal with these types of people who set out to ruin others' days? Robert Sutton, PhD, in *The No Asshole Rule: Building a Civilized Workplace and Surviving One That Isn't,* shares his list of the top twelve results of allowing a jerk's obnoxious behavior to invade the workplace. Are any of these common annoyances evident in your office or workplace?

The Dirty Dozen

Personal insults

Invading coworkers' personal territory

Uninvited physical contact

Threats and intimidation, verbal or nonverbal

Sarcastic jokes and teasing

Withering e-mails

Treating people as if they were invisible

Status slaps

Public shaming

Rude interruptions

Two-faced attacks

Dirty looks

Sutton says there is a cost to having jerks in the office. The list illustrates the includibly effective bottom line results of getting rid of jerks and jerkiness in the office. Imagine not having to have a budget for these residual expenses.

Possible Effects That Contribute to TCJ (Total Cost of Jerks)

Distraction from tasks

Fear of speaking up

Turnover

Legal costs

Time spent appeasing or reorganizing

Anger management training

Reduction in innovation

Retaliation

So, what can you do about someone whose apparent "jerkiness" in the office scores a ten on your annoyance meter? If you feel strong enough, you can confront the person. If you feel that you need a little backup, you can talk to your supervisor about how best to approach the situation. Perhaps posting signs about proper office etiquette or other such "friendly reminders" in places such as the bathroom, kitchen, and common spaces might make a difference. Just remember: You cannot always control the behavior of others, so why let them take control of your life? Don't be annoyed—just be thankful that you don't go through life being a jerk.

Notes

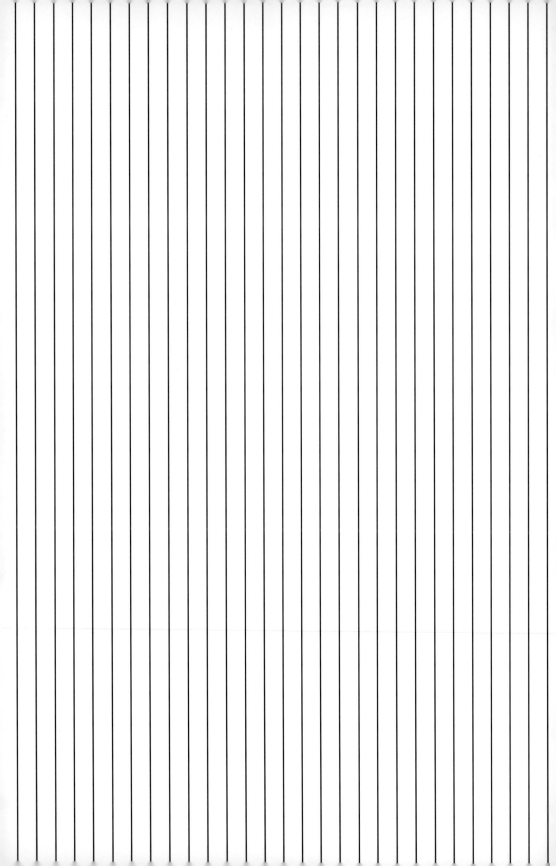

CHAPTER 4

BEING SERVED

Every day, we venture out into the world and encounter other people. Many times, we interact with these other people in a standard customer service relationship—whether it is at a restaurant, in a department store, or on a tech support line. Just as with our families or friends, there are definite annoyances that come via the customer service territory. Learning how to effectively quell these frustrations will make our interactions with strangers much more manageable and pleasant.

General Customer Service

Virtual Help Desks

> "The problem when calling a help desk for a
> computer question, product recall, or other
> knowledge issues is that the agents don't speak
> clearly enough for me to understand them."
>
> —*Various people*

With American companies outsourcing to Asia for their call centers, this is understandable. Most Americans only speak English and only hear it spoken in their hometown, on television, or in the movies. When native English speakers call for assistance and talk with a person who speaks English with an unfamiliar accent, these callers sometimes choose to not understand. *The Solution:* If you call a help desk and have difficulty understanding the person on the other line, ask him to please slow down and don't be afraid to ask him to repeat something. After all, you are calling to get help and it's understandable that you may not grasp the information on the first try. However, it is somewhat pointless to get annoyed because you can't change who you are talking to. So just pay more attention to the words and ask for clarification when needed. The important thing is to not accuse the agent of being difficult. Take responsibility. You will foster greater positive communication if you tell the person that the difficulty with the communication is your fault.

"It's annoying when customer service reps fail to carefully read your question during a live chat and answer a completely different question."

—*Anonymous*

The Solution: After reading some of these chats, it is apparent that the questioner needs to use clearer language when asking his question. When we don't have a live person sitting in front of us to chat with, the words we use are even more important for relaying our question to the agent. Many people have difficulty with written language and there is often a comprehension gap between client and agent. Both sides are most likely frustrated but there is little that can be done to solve this problem. So, just be careful how you word your question and try to practice a little more patience when you receive a faulty answer.

The Doctor's Office

The number-one issue complainers have with doctors is long office waits. We make appointments expecting that we will be seen during a specific time period—between the time of our appointment and an hour thereafter. Yet, people clearly find themselves waiting unbelievable amounts of time to see a doctor, even when they have a scheduled appointment.

"When I visit my doctor, I'm often ushered into a small, private room and asked to wait there even after I've waited for more than thirty minutes past my appointment. Then, twenty minutes later the doctor comes in and doesn't even apologize. Even if he does, my frustration level has raised my blood pressure and made the whole experience tainted."

—*Joy B. from Dallas, Texas*

When we are imposed upon to the point of frustration, we don't listen to the practitioner as closely, or we disregard what he says entirely because he has lost our trust. We based our trust on his respect for us as patients (clients). Wasting our time with no or inadequate explanation is not acceptable. ***The Solution:*** Speak up for yourself! When was the last time you said something to your doctor about his tardiness? We hold doctors in high esteem which, for many, makes it difficult to talk with them about their behavior flaws. They too, are suppliers of services that we pay for. If you have a problem with their demeanor, you should say something. I have told physicians who make me wait the following: "I know you are busy today, but my appointment was at 2 pm and it is now 3:20 pm. I received no explanation for the long wait and your tardiness has caused me to have to juggle my already tight schedule. I don't appreciate that. In the future, if I am asked to wait more than fifteen minutes, I will leave and I will not pay for the appointment." This particular doctor looked at me with respect and embarrassment and apologized. I also heard him say to his staff as I was leaving that if anyone has to wait longer than fifteen or twenty minutes for their appointment, please ask them if they are willing to do so or reschedule them. Sometimes sticking up for oneself does change the annoying behaviors of others for the better.

Not only do customers expect to be treated with good behavior and proper etiquette but the same goes for the other side of the desk.

> "Patients who give the doctor's office their middle name instead of their legal name, then get upset at the doctor's office because the insurance has no clue who you are is very frustrating!"
>
> —*Doctor's office receptionist*

The Solution: If you find this to be a common problem, ask the patient for their full "legal" name. This should clue him in to the fact that you need both his first and middle names and then you shouldn't encounter the frustrations linked to insurance troubles.

> "Patients who come in early for their appointment and expect to be seen in front of the patients who are already in the office are rude!"
>
> —*Several front desk employees in doctors' offices*

There are many people who feel their time is more precious than the rest of the population. There are certain rules that we learn about taking turns and about what is fair. These patients believe that if they are present at the office, they should be served immediately. **The Solution:** A gentle reminder such as, "We are glad you are here on time but we have to see those whose appointments were scheduled earlier than yours. I know you understand the fairness of that" should at least make you feel as though you've staved off this annoyance (even if the "entitled" person doesn't like your response).

Retail

From the Store's Point of View

There are complaints about customers just as there are complaints about clerks in retail stores. We should understand that interactions only go well if both parties are able to relate with patience, good manners, and friendliness.

Key Complaints (from store clerks)

Customers who come into stores for the pure entertainment value of trying on clothes or playing with items with no intention of buying anything

Many customers do not say "Thank you," "Excuse me," or "Please."

Customers who insist that you open a package to see what is clearly illustrated on the outside

Customers who ask questions of the clerk who is standing on a high ladder (this compromises the clerk's safety)

Parents who send their kids into stores, thinking the sales clerks will entertain them (with video games, clothes, toys) while the parents visit different stores

Clerks feeling as if they are treated like babysitters

Children who are allowed to use "skate shoes" inside stores

"Parents who let their kids take toys out of the box at the store and let them play with the toys that they don't plan on buying [are so frustrating]."

—*An anonymous sales clerk in a popular childrens toy store*

This is certainly a problem because it requires the clerk to repackage the toys so they are still in salable condition (if the box is completely destroyed, then the store loses a profit). ***The Solution:*** If you are a store clerk and you see a parent allowing this to happen, either alert your store manager to the situation or, if you feel comfortable enough, approach the parent and tell him that it is against store policy for toys to be opened before being purchased. Ask him if he'd like you to ring up the toy for him and watch as the behavior ends. Take control of these situations so you do not get annoyed and can teach people a valuable lesson.

> "Parents who let their children scream and make loud noises in the store [are annoying and ruin the atmosphere of the store]."
>
> —*Some store clerks and managers*

Parents who don't control their children while shopping put the store's employees in a difficult position. ***The Solution:*** If you work at a store and this situation occurs, you need to say something to the parents about the noise, but do so in a professional way so as not to insult the customer. Most parents will try to oblige you and will remind their children to keep their voices down. Keep in mind that when criticizing someone, you achieve your goal faster if you compliment or empathize with the offending party before you say something negative. Also, the best procedure is to criticize quietly and away from other shoppers rather than in front of a crowd, where the offender might be judged and feel embarrassed.

Key Complaints (from the customers)

Not greeted properly by the sales clerk

Not given the common courtesy of a "Please" or "Thank you" when checking out

Sales clerk makes me feel intrusive for shopping in their store

From the Customer's Point of View

The sales personnel we encounter in a store often create the experience we have in that store and ultimately encourage or discourage us from returning to shop there. The clerks who wait on us can be the store's greatest marketing advantage or they could, with their annoying and bad behavior, be the reason the store will soon cease to exist.

> "I'm annoyed when a store clerk comes up to me and asks how my day is going."
>
> —*Anonymous customer*

I suppose there are some people who interpret general kindness as being a personal affront. However, a friendly greeting such as this should be accepted as part of the normal interaction between clerk and customer. ***The Solution:*** Try to enjoy the interaction. The clerk is not out to ruin your day by being friendly. A simple "Hello" from you and a "No thanks, I'm just looking" will deter him from asking you anything more and will leave you in peace.

> "[I'm annoyed by] clerks who ignore me."
>
> —*Many customers*

In many cases, these employees are trying not to intrude on your shopping unless you seem to need assistance. It is difficult for many

---

What We Don't Want to See at the Checkout

- Clerks chewing gum with an open mouth
- Clerks on a personal call while waiting on me
- Not enough checkout clerks at grocery stores
- Store clerks who insult another employee in front of customers
- Clerks who act like you are disturbing them if you ask for assistance

- Store clerks doing business on the phone while you wait to pay
- Clerks who are too busy talking to each other to serve you
- Store clerks who let pushy customers cut in front of others
- Nagging sales clerks
- Sales clerks who complain about their jobs in front of customers
- Clerks who know less about the product than I do
- Clerks who don't even acknowledge you are there
- Clerks who complain about customers right in front of you
- When stores clerks don't say "Thank you"
- Clerks who say *nothing* to you at all. Not "Hi," or the total due, or "please" and "thank you." How rude!

clerks to assess what the customer might find acceptable as far as approaching him is concerned. Personally, I like to remain anonymous in a store until I need some assistance. Then I want a clerk close by who is willing and able to assist me in a friendly way. That said, I suggest that if you are ignored by a clerk, be assertive and go up to him, ask how he is doing, and then implore his help. This should do the trick in most cases.

Customers Annoying Other Customers

Our experience shopping in a store doesn't stop with the sales clerks or managers. Often our complaints come from the other shoppers and our expectations for how they should behave in stores.

"All the people who flock to the stores before a storm to buy milk, bread, and toilet paper [annoy me]! If they'd keep these things in stock there wouldn't be such a mad rush to the store!"

—*Lisa G. from Chicago*

The Solution: Take a deep breath and move on because, in all honesty, wishing others would live their lives the way you live yours is not realistic. We all have so many individual circumstances to deal with that judging others by the standards we employ will only bring unnecessary frustration.

"People in grocery stores who check out in the express line where you're only supposed to have twelve items or less and they've got a cart full of stuff [are very annoying]."

—*Annoyed people in the grocery store*

The Solution: If the line is long and you see someone in front of you with a huge pile of groceries, you could politely excuse yourself and alert him to the fact that he is in the express lane. Perhaps he just didn't read the signs. Or, if other lanes look free, just take your purchase to one of those open lanes—just because you have twelve items or fewer doesn't mean you cannot check out in a regular lane (and if it saves you the annoyance, it's well worth it).

Another kindness would be to notice if the person behind you in a regular line has only one item and you have many. Give up your place to that person. I do this whenever possible and it makes both me and the other shopper have a better day.

"[It's frustrating when you encounter] people in stores who take up the whole width of an aisle talking to others and do not make room for others to get by or to get what they want off a shelf."

—*Anonymous customers*

Self-absorption is common in our day and age. **The Solution:** It's really quite simple. Just say "Excuse me, I'm trying to get through" or "Excuse me, but I need to reach the cereal on the shelf right above you." Take charge of your own destiny and then you won't find yourself getting so annoyed at these small inconveniences.

"I don't understand why people can't walk the twenty-five or thirty feet to return their shopping carts to the proper place rather than leaving them in the parking lot where they run into cars.

—Desiree Powell

I have to agree with this annoyance, especially because my car was seriously damaged by a runaway cart left on an incline. Not only the potential damage to cars but also the parking places that are taken up by the carts when the lot is full can be infuriating to those trying to park. Add to that inclement weather, the shoppers' moods as they find a parking place, and go into the store and your shopping experience might be seriously hindered. ***The Solution:*** If you are heading into a shop, offer to take the cart from the other person and use it for your own shopping. And, if you see a cart in a parking space or on a treacherous incline, be a Good Samaritan and return it. Don't expect people to have manners—but don't let them ruin your or anyone else's day either.

Restaurants

Eating out can be pleasant or not depending upon the people you are eating with and their habits (as we discussed in chapter 2). Furthermore, the restaurant you choose and its staff, food, and atmosphere also are factors in our enjoyment of a restaurant meal. When we decide to eat out, we are always conscious of the cost of the experience. We want to be sure the experience is commensurate with the money and time we spend on it. We have control over what we choose from the menu but there are so many other variables. We depend upon the restaurant to provide a positive overall experience for us.

The Customer vs. the Waitstaff

"Dirty silverware at a restaurant is gross and annoying."

—Common diners' complaint

There is no excuse for this. Setting the table with dirty utensils should never be allowed. *The Solution:* If you find soiled utensils, don't make a big deal about it by commenting out loud to your table-mates. Instead, ask the waiter for another piece of silverware and enjoy your meal. As the diner, your reaction to others' mistakes influences how others perceive you in all things you do.

> "People who lick their plates in restaurants are really annoying."
>
> —*Anonymous*

What are people thinking? *The Solution:* Try to concentrate on your own plate and that of anyone who is eating with you and keep your eyes off the other diners. That's the best advice I can give.

> "People who take too long to order at a restaurant or keep changing their mind [are frustrating beyond belief]."
>
> —*Common complaint among both diners and waitstaff*

If you are in this situation, obviously you are dealing with someone who has trouble making up his mind. *The Solution:* Why not be helpful rather than annoyed? Make some suggestions and sell a dish. The undecided diner only wants something that he believes will be tasty.

> "Being invited to a birthday dinner at an expensive restaurant only to learn at the end that you are expected to chip in to pay the bill is a huge pet peeve."
>
> —*Annoyed birthday guests*

This is a situation encountered by many who don't ask the pertinent questions when they respond to an invitation. *The Solution:* To avoid this situation, ask who the host is and whether guests are expected to pay anything. If the answer is yes to sharing expenses, you have the choice to say, "No but thank you for the invitation." It is a grievous etiquette error to invite someone to an event and expect them to pay for anything and if you don't feel you want to help out with the bill, you don't need to celebrate with the birthday person.

"Getting the bill to come to the right person [i.e., me] at the end of the meal is very frustrating and awkward."

—*Anonymous*

Paying the bill at the end of the meal can add quite a few annoyances. *The Solution:* If you want to pay the bill at the end of the meal, make it clear to the waiter ahead of time. Tell him, at the beginning of the meal, that you'd like the check at the end. Better yet, if you don't want the bill to even come to the table, alert the manager as you enter the restaurant, have him run your credit card (and return it to you before you sit down), and explain that you will sign the receipt as you leave. This is a savvy and common way to be a gracious host.

"I despise when the waiter takes the check and money from me and asks if I need change."

—*Sally F. from San Jose, California*

It seems like a typical question from waiters, even though you might have already done the right thing and figured in the tip with the charges and given the total to the waiter. *The Solution:* So there is no confusion on the waiter's part (and no annoyance on yours) as you hand the payment back, tell the waiter if you need any change.

"I dislike it when my friends don't tip the waitstaff, for whatever reason."

—*Annoyed friend*

The Solution: If you notice your friends doing this and you feel that you would like to leave a gratuity, you are well within good etiquette to do so. But don't talk about it with the person who paid the bill because you will most likely provoke a defensive response. Consider it your random act of kindness for the day. And if you see this as repeated behavior on your friend's part, perhaps discuss it outside of the restaurant or just stop going out to eat with him.

> "[I'm annoyed by] waiters who hover like vultures and who talk with you as if they are part of the party."
>
> —*Joe Williams from New York*

The Solution: If this is a problem, a kind comment such as, "We appreciate your attentive service but we need some privacy right now" will take care of the problem. We need to inform overly aggressive or friendly staff that the best way to serve us is to wait until we signal for them.

> "When waiters say, 'Enjoy' as they leave your order on the table [it is bothersome]."
>
> —*Many people*

The Solution: Smile and take it as a friendly gesture. Some people, however, take it as a sarcastic comment that grates on their nerves. If it irritates you, understand it is probably not meant to be sarcastic.

> "I despise waiters/waitresses who never check on you after your meal is served! The waiters who give you menus at a restaurant and leave and you never see them for an hour ruin our meal!!! Additionally, I have gotten up and gotten coffee and poured it for us and other people and the waiter [then] gives me a dirty look."
>
> —*Steve G. from Arlington, Virginia*

Of course what the waiter should have done in the above instance is come to your table, apologize, and then give you amazing service for the rest of your meal, though I rarely see that happen. *The Solution:* If you are able to make eye contact with a member of the waitstaff, signal him over and tell him that you feel you are being ignored and then ask him for whatever you need. If no one is to be found, leave your seat and get a manager. I have found that doing this makes the rest of the service extra special.

> "When you sit down at a restaurant and the waitress says, 'How are you *guys* tonight?' really irks me."
>
> —*Many female diners*

This is a legitimate complaint. We are not all "guys"—there are some ladies in our group. This type of greeting is a casual approach by the waitstaff and thus lacks formal respect for others. It falls in the same category of immediately calling someone by their given name upon meeting them. Of course, depending upon the area of the world in which you live, there are variations on this theme. We are also not folks, buckaroos, kids, people, or gals. A simple, "Good evening. I am glad you are here. I am _____ and I will be your server tonight" would set the tone much better and make everyone feel welcome. ***The Solution:*** If you are put in this position and are annoyed by it, follow the lead of a woman I know. Say, "I am a lady and so is my friend. If we are guys, our husbands have a shock in store for them. Please don't call us guys." The waitress, when told this, was a little taken aback but she smiled and responded with, "You are so right! What drinks may I get for you ladies tonight?" This was a classic example of teaching others how to treat us. I applaud this waitress for understanding that what she said seemed condescending to her customers. So try this approach and hopefully you will receive a similar, respectful response.

The Waitstaff vs. the Customer

Many waiters and waitresses complain just as often about their customers.

> "Guests who won't get off their cell phone, even when I am standing in front of them waiting to take their order [are very annoying]."
>
> —*Common waitstaff complaint*

The Solution: If I were the waitress I would stand there until I made eye contact, smile, and say, "Excuse me. Are you ready to order?" If I got no response, I would back off and return in three minutes or continue around the table and take the others' orders, hoping the cell phone addict would catch on.

"People who are rude to service workers are obnoxious to be around."

—*Anonymous Service Worker*

I agree. You learn quite a bit about someone by how he treats people who serve him. If he is respectful and kind to waitstaff and retail clerks, his character is strong and most likely ethical. If he is not, he would likely not be the person you would want to work or socialize with. ***The Solution:*** If you are the service worker and are being mistreated, you don't need to just stand there and take it. You can either alert your manager to the disrespectful behavior or you can confront the perpetrator yourself. Stick up for yourself. If you are with someone who is rude to a service worker, tell him that the behavior is rude and, if you find a chance, you could always apologize for your friend's bad behavior. And then I'd suggest that you stop going out with him in social settings.

Fast-food Industry

"Fast food isn't fast."

—*People across the country*

There were a lot of comments about the fast-food side of the restaurant industry. We patronize a fast-food establishment because we don't have the time to sit down at a table and be served. But we have even stricter expectations when the word "fast" is associated with our meal. We expect to be in and out in the blink of an eye. And in the middle of the blink we want our fellow patrons to be as quick, clean, respectful, and efficient as we believe we are. The problem is that they aren't. We encounter people in fast-food establishments who have never eaten at a white tablecloth restaurant and their behavior is what we might call "a little rough around the edges." There are some expectations from diners at these restaurants, however, that should be considered and annoyances that we should squelch.

> "[I'm easily annoyed by] people in fast-food lines who do not look up at the menu until the cashier says 'May I take your order?' and also when someone stands in line at a fast-food place with their kids, waiting ten minutes. Then they get up there and ask their kids 'What do you want?' Why didn't they ask their kids while they were waiting in line?"
>
> —*B. Welsh from New York*

Usually when I witness this, there is a fight about what the kids may have according to their mother versus what they really want. So the transaction takes another five minutes. When you are in hurry and hungry, this translates into eternity. ***The Solution:*** Calm down and wait your turn. And be sure you don't do the same thing to the person behind you.

> "I'm frustrated with the lack of training in these [fast-food] places. The clerks can't get the order right or they can't count change correctly or they just don't act pleasant and glad to serve you."
>
> —*Anonymous complaint*

The Solution: As the patron, it just takes a bit more patience to make the experience endurable. Keep in mind that many of the employees are young and inexperienced with working with the public and your visible frustration will surely make them even more nervous, affecting their service.

"In the drive-through, [fast-food restaurant managers] always seem to put someone on the intercom who can't speak English!"

—Julio Gomez from Arizona

It seems obvious that good business practice dictates having some-one who clearly speaks the native language taking orders. However, the public is quite judgmental about people who speak with accents. Many of us are not raised in towns where we might hear a Hispanic or Chinese or Russian accent. The speaker is speaking English well enough, but we don't recognize it as such because of their unfamil-iar accent. ***The Solution:*** This peeve is really about one's inability to understand because of his *own* lack of experience with others from dif-ferent cultures, not the mispronunciation of the language by someone from another culture. Ask for clarification of your order. Learn to show empathy, not annoyance, and know that you will soon be getting your meal—it just might take a little more patience than you normally have.

"People who go to a fast-food restaurant and have an order as long as your arm, needing each item custom made, are annoying."

—Anonymous fast-food patrons

Of course, we all know that the patron with the order should move to the side out of the general line because the order will obviously take a long time to fill. However, not everyone acts with the same level of courtesy. ***The Solution:*** If there is another line you can get into then do so. If not, just take a deep breath and know that you'll soon get your turn to order.

"[It's frustrating when] people assume you are less than human because you work in the fast-food industry."

—Mark from London UK

I agree with this lament. A job in a fast-food restaurant is still an honest job and should be respected. Unfortunately, these jobs have been mocked by comedians and those who work in high-end establishments as being the bottom rung of the employment ladder. I disagree. Anyone who feels this way should try it for a few days and see how they handle the people, the demands, the rudeness from patrons, and the hectic pace that is common. ***The Solution:*** If someone ever approaches you and says something snotty to you about your fast-food job, you should feel confident enough to tell him that you don't appreciate his snide remark—that you work just as hard as anyone else. There will always be people out there who look down on others; just know that it is a self-esteem issue for the person and be thankful that you are much more open-minded in your view of the world.

Random Acts of Fast-Food Annoyances

I have favorite pet peeves sent in from readers and among them is this one:

> "I hate pushing all the little dents on the top of fast-food drink lids."
>
> —*Anonymous*

It is a little tricky the first time, but if you have been drinking from disposable cups provided by fast-food establishments, you should have the hang of this already. If not, ask a child. They will be happy to show you how it's done.

> "When overweight people go into a fast-food establishment, order a super-sized meal, and then have the nerve to order a DIET soda! What a crock!"
>
> —*Mean-spirited people*

Well, in all honesty, a Diet Coke does cut down on the total calorie count. And if you are so shallow as to find this a grievous annoyance, then you probably should stop going to fast-food restaurants yourself. Most patrons don't seek out fast-food for a healthy meal.

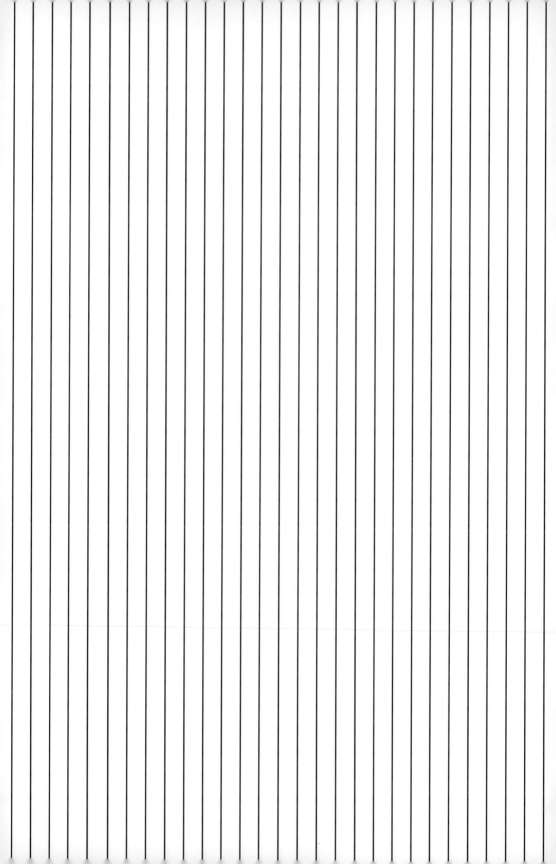

CHAPTER 5

PLUGGED IN

We live in a digital age that is increasingly dependent on technology and instant communication. Using telephones, cell phones, and e-mail, we are able to communicate with people from almost every possible location. This luxury, however, comes with a price: These devices are just portals for more annoying behavior to leak through. It is important to manage our annoyances within these mediums in order to continue to enjoy this modern age and to lower our stress levels.

Telephones

The telephone is the perfect example of where the difference between a request and a demand come into play. We also don't have the benefit of body language to help us interpret the intent and mood of the other person with whom we are speaking. Therefore his words and tone of voice are our only guides. Because approximately sixty percent of our understanding of a message is gained by interpretation of body language, we are at a disadvantage when speaking on the telephone. Indicators such as grumpy, tired, sick, happy, joyful, and defensive come out in our voices. When we talk on the phone with others, it is easy to become frustrated or annoyed, depending on the conversation we are having or the circumstances we are under while talking to the other person. Learning how to react to these telephone conversation annoyances will help us become happier and less frustrated every day of our lives.

"At work we clearly identify ourselves when we answer a call by saying, 'Dr Smith's office. How may I help you?' The customer replies, 'Is this Dr. Smith's office?' AHH! That's what I just said."

—Terry

Understanding how the human mind works will help ease some of this frustration. When we first hear words coming from the other end of the phone, we register it as noise—either friendly or not. "Good morning," "Good afternoon," and "Good evening" are all friendly noises. "Hello" is neither friendly nor abusive so we cannot judge if we will be taken care of by the person who answered. We don't start listening to the words until the second sentence. Because in this example there was no friendly noise to prompt the caller to start listening, the customer doesn't start listening for words and meaning until "How may I help you?" ***The Solution:*** If you are tired of being asked a redundant question on the phone, add an opening sentence that will be either heard or not and then state the pertinent information in the second sentence. That way, the listener will hear what you want him to hear, and you won't need to repeat a thing.

"We have a recording [at our office] letting people know our business hours and yet people will still call to ask our hours! [So annoying!]"

—Mark V

The Solution: In all honesty, people don't listen to recordings, so they will continue to ask questions about business hours. Just realize that it's part of the job.

"We'll let a customer know Mike is gone for the day yet a customer will still ask if they can speak to him! Grr!"

—*Bill Williams from Biloxi, MS*

Again, assume nobody is listening. ***The Solution:*** Tell the caller that Mike is gone for the day and then ask the caller for an active response. Ask if he would like to be transferred to Mike's voicemail or if you could take a message for him. Many people stop thinking if they are not given a choice.

"I can't stand it when someone is talking with me and then just hangs up. No goodbye. I am left wondering if the conversation is really over or if we got disconnected."

—*Cynthia Lett*

Yes, this is my own, personal annoyance when communicating by phone. ***The Solution:*** If I initiate the call and am not certain it's been mutually completed, I will call back to check. The etiquette rule is that if you say hello, you must say goodbye.

"I'm annoyed when people screen calls. We are asked, 'May I tell him what your call is regarding?' when we feel it is none of the operator's or secretary's business why we are calling."

—*Many annoyed callers*

The Solution: If you adopt a proper method of making the call, being screened won't happen as often. When we call someone, the first thing we should say is our full name, slowly enough for the other person to understand it. Then we need to identify our affiliation. For instance, "This is Cynthia Lett from The Lett Group." The proper etiquette rule for making a request rather than a demand should come into play at this point. Most people will say, "Is George Miller there?" when they should be asking, "Is George Miller available?" It really doesn't matter if Mr. Miller is there if he is not available. He could be there but in a meeting, in the kitchen, in the bathroom, or chatting with coworkers. To cut the possibility of being sent to voice-mail because the person answering doesn't believe you are important enough to talk with Mr. Miller, you might add, "I am returning his call." Or "I am following up on our last meeting." Or "I was referred to him by a friend of his at another company." Of course whatever further information you give, it needs to be the truth or you will be caught and judged immediately as a liar or too aggressive. If you are told he is not available, by all means ask if you can leave a message in his voicemail.

Cell Phones

General Cell Phone Annoyances

The phone going off in a(n):

Restaurant

Church

Class

Movie

Car

Museum/Gallery

Concert/Performance

Elevator

Meeting

Subway

The number one annoyance I received was "Everyone else's cell phone!" many offered several examples of their frustrations throughout various life situations, but everyone listed the cell phone as their main annoyance.

"Being trapped in a car while someone has a lengthy cell phone conversation is such an intrusion into my privacy. It makes me have to intrude into theirs and it is just rude!"

—*Susan Pumphrey from Arlington, VA*

Being trapped in a place while someone is having a cell phone conversation feels intrusive and embarrassing to everyone. We feel that we shouldn't be listening, that our voyeuristic interests shouldn't be fulfilled, and that we are being forced to listen in on a private conversation. So, what do you do when you are the victim of cell phone intrusion? ***The Solution:*** As much as you would hope to change someone's cell phone behavior, understand that you won't be able to. Most of us know how rude it is to talk in front of others, disturbing the quiet and calm. Many don't care to change how they handle it when their cell phone rings. You won't be able to stop their rudeness, so give them alternatives to disturbing you. Don't stew; don't roll your eyes while staring at the intruder. Don't mutter under your breath or worse, out loud. Interrupt with a smile. Say, "I know you would prefer some privacy for your call. Would you mind stepping away?" Offer to hold their place if you are in a waiting room, in line, or other place.

"I get really peeved when someone's cell phone goes off during a meal at a restaurant."

—*Anonymous diner*

The Solution: In a restaurant when you are dining with others, you could try setting the tone at your table by announcing that you are turning off your cell phone because your company is more important to you right now than any call that might be come. You are not directly telling them to do the same thing, but by assuming this leadership position you are inferring that if they don't do the same, they are showing that you aren't so important.

> ### "I hate it when people talk on cell phones (usually loudly) in the elevator!"
> —*Annoyed elevator rider*

The Solution: If someone enters the elevator while on a call there isn't much you can say without attacking the rude rider. In the past, after getting off the elevator, I told someone who loudly held a conversation for all to hear during our ride that I never ride and talk because I don't want strangers to hear my private conversations. I never know who might be listening and it could hurt me. I share the lesson by using myself as the example, rather than the perpetrator of the annoyance.

> ### "It's appalling and annoying when someone's cell phone rings during church service."
> —*Churchgoer*

You would think that the pure embarrassment of having your cell phone ring during a religious service would be enough for the owner to learn to remember to turn it off. After all, who could be calling who is more important than God? Most likely the annoyed looks of fellow parishioners will be enough to teach that lesson. However, I have heard of ministers and rabbis who have had to make announcements regarding the rules of quiet needed to respect all who are present. **The Solution:** Well, after all, you are in a place where everyone is asking for forgiveness for everything else they have or have not done—so forgive the person whose cell phone just interrupted the service and don't hold a grudge against them.

E-mail

In keeping with the times, e-mail pet peeves ranked high. There are so many rules that we never learned about e-mail that will eventually get us into trouble—with our bosses, with our friends, with the law.

"People who don't read their e-mail annoy me."

—*Anonymous*

The Solution: If you know that someone is lax about reading his e-mail and what you have to tell him is important, by all means don't rely on e-mail to send the message. Phones work all over the world.

"Chain letter junkies are very obnoxious—the people who forward those stupid e-mails to everyone on their friends list and if you don't follow suit you'll have whatever many years bad luck."

—*Victim of too many "forwards"*

The Solution: There is no written rule that you have to forward these (and do you really believe you'll have bad luck if you don't?). I also respond to the senders and say that I appreciate their thinking of me but I will never follow up with these so it might be best to take me off their chain e-mail list.

"E-mail being used in place of face-to-face communication is bothersome to me."

—*Anonymous*

There was a study done in 2004 that compared how many trusted friends Americans had in 1984 and in 2004. The number was three in 1984; the number in 2004 was generally one. My conclusion from this data is that it is impossible to have a trusted friend whom you never actually see or talk with. E-mail has come to be our main mode of conversation and our personal relationships are suffering as a result. ***The Solution:*** Call a friend or arrange a meeting for an hour or two. Your relationship will become stronger each time you do this. With e-mail, you don't have the advantage of reading body language which more forcefully shows how a person feels about you than your words ever will.

Important Things to Consider About E-mail

1. It never dies. Once written and sent, every e-mail ever written will be kept somewhere. They are easily retrievable and can easily get us into a lot of trouble.
2. They are supposed to be letters that don't require stamps, envelopes, paper, and ink. They are not memos. They are not text messages. They are not conversations. They are letters that should start with a salutation (Dear Mr. Jones), contain coherent thoughts, and end with a closing (Sincerely, Mary Johnson). When was the last time you received an e-mail that looked like a properly written letter?
3. They should be free of spelling mistakes, abbreviations, and slang.
4. They should be civil. Emotion and temper should never be a part of an e-mail.
5. They should be worth the time we spend reading them. Cluttering someone's inbox is stealing precious time from that person's life. Do we have the right to do that?
6. E-mails are not for conflict resolution.
7. Never go more than two rounds on e-mail. If you need more than two e-mails to make a point, negotiate a deal, answer a concern, or fix any problem, do what truly successful professionals do— pick up the phone and have a conversation.
8. Assume everyone will read the e-mail. Not only do e-mails last forever, they can be read by everyone on earth who possesses an e-mail account. The cc and bcc fields are dangerous. We don't know to whom the recipient will send a copy of the e-mail. Do we really know the recipient well enough to trust that the e-mail will remain for his eyes only?
9. Change the subject line as the content changes. How many times have you received an e-mail that shows a subject line relevant to the initial question at hand but totally unrelated to the current content of the e-mail? We have to search our inbox for items

we immediately need to read and an irrelevant subject line will cause us to miss important information. A subject line should be the same as what you would say when starting a conversation with the recipient. Examples of good subject lines: Prices for your next order; *Time reset for this afternoon's meeting; Inquiry about your services; Question from Bob Smith.* All of these subject lines inform the reader of the contents of the e-mail.

"Spam and junk e-mails are the most annoying things ever!"

—Many anonymous e-mailers

Oh, how we hate (not dislike, hate) spam! Fortunately, in our ever evolving technologically savvy times, spam blockers are getting better. Until they are as intuitive as the human mind, we will have to put up with junk mail. ***The Solution:*** The one thing you can control about spam is not sending it. I personally had the unfortunate problem of a hacker getting my e-mail off of my Web site and using it to send sexually explicit spam to people I will never know or meet. Fortunately I heard from some people who asked if I knew that it had been done. I immediately sent an e-mail to anyone on my mailing list who may have received this spam apologizing for the invasion and explaining it was not sent by me but by a hacker. Everyone who responded understood because such is the nature of the times we live in. They all appreciated that I was proactive with my apology and no harm was done.

"When I am reading an e-mail and someone else comes up and starts reading it too, I get annoyed."

—Anonymous

The Solution: Just look at the person and kindly say, "I'm sorry but this is my personal e-mail and I'd rather you not read it." Or, if you can exit your e-mail, do so and wait until the person is gone.

"I can't stand forwards, forwards, and more forwards."

—Sierra C.

This is totally understandable. If it is necessary to forward an e-mail so another person can receive the same information, the proper thing to do is to inform the original sender that you are forwarding his e-mail and to whom. ***The Solution:*** If you have one friend who is a "forwarding addict," write him a simple e-mail requesting that he not send you any forwards as you don't have time to read them. You can also just refuse to open them, and simply delete them. A simple mouse click will make that particular annoyance disappear.

"People who capitalize everything in an e-mail are annoying!"

—Incredible number of e-mail users

Netiquette rules state that capitalizing is the same as SHOUTING. It also shows great laziness if the writer can't be bothered to release the caps lock key with one finger stroke. ***The Solution:*** Write the culprit a sweet e-mail saying that it is hard to read his e-mails when the message is in all capital letters. Beyond that, just understand that some people don't understand the rules of e-mail and that it's really not the end of the world.

"People who don't remove all of the other addresses at the beginning of their e-mail before they send it on to you are irksome."

—Anonymous

Hundreds of people submitted this same peeve. This breach of netiquette is not only annoying to many but puts the burden of a possible breach of security on the shoulders of the sender. All of the e-mail addresses that are forwarded are now available for future use, perhaps for unethical purposes. ***The Solution:*** Show your concern about the increase of spam by removing e-mail addresses the recipients should not be privy to and remind the person who sent along the unedited e-mail to do the same next time.

> "People who use abbreviations in e-mails instead of just spelling out the words drive me crazy [as do] people who use Internet slang in company/official e-mails (lol)."
>
> —*Alex P. from Camden, NJ*

The Solution: The first time someone does this, the best approach is to say something such as, "I know how easy it is to write in code, but as a slow decoder, it would be easier for me to read your e-mails if you would spell it all out for me." The key is to inform the writer of what works for you so that your communication will work for both of you.

> "I'm annoyed by people who get upset with you for not answering an e-mail the second you get it."
>
> —*Various e-mailers*

The Solution: The etiquette rule for answering e-mails is twenty-four hours if it is business related and forty-eight hours if it is personal. If your e-mail is complicated or requires some thought before a true response, send a quick reply saying, "I received your e-mail and will get back to you tomorrow morning after I've given some thought to my response." We all need to feel we are not being ignored—and this will help put the sender and you at ease.

Voicemail

Key Complaints

1. People who talk too fast and I can't hear clearly their name or phone number—this requires me to hit play over and over and it is just not worth it

2. People who don't leave their name

3. People who don't leave their number

4. People who conduct a complete sales pitch in one voicemail

5. Hearing, "Call me" and nothing else—the caller expects me to recognize their voice and assumes I have the number

6. Not leaving a reason for the call—I don't know who they are or why I would call them back

7. Giving too much information

8. Ranting and raving and then not leaving their personal information

9. People who speak with an accent and don't spell their last name so I know I have it right

Voicemail is a helpful tool that most people use incorrectly. Just about everyone who submitted an annoyance included voicemail. The list of frustrations above can be solved by following these few common tips concerning voicemail etiquette. *The Solution:* Start by speaking more slowly than you usually do over the phone. Give your name, spell your last name slowly, say your phone number and pause after every three or four numbers so the listener can write it down, give your affiliation and reason for the call, repeat your name and phone number, and name a good time to return your call. As an example, I leave messages like this: "This is Cynthia Lett—L-E-T-T—of The Lett Group. My number is 301-946-8208. I am responding to your inquiry about seminars on business etiquette that you sent by e-mail this morning. I will be in my office this afternoon until 5 pm and again tomorrow until noon. Again, this is Cynthia Lett at 301-946-8208. I look forward to our conversation. Goodbye."

"People who hang up before they leave a voicemail because they expected to talk to me are a big annoyance."

—*Anonymous*

This isn't such a bad thing in my estimation. ***The Solution:*** If your caller didn't have anything important to say to you, then it seems just as well that he doesn't waste your time with listening to a voicemail message that doesn't say anything. If he has something to tell you, he'll call back at another time, so no need to sweat or fret.

Caller ID

There are plenty of pet peeves that involve caller ID as well as questions about whether you can use that information to further your own agenda with a person. Connie from Florida shared that when she sees that on her caller ID a friend has called but her friend did not leave a message, she is flummoxed about whether it is good etiquette to call her back and say, "I see that you called. What's going on?" There are no standard etiquette rules concerning caller ID yet. The common-sense answer is that if someone didn't leave a message, which is an intentional signal that he called and wants a return call from you, you are not supposed to call him back. If you are the one to call and not leave a message, know that according to several law enforcement officers it could be considered stalking if someone calls repeatedly and doesn't leave a message. So even if you think you are anonymous, you can be found out. Of course, if this person is a friend, and you would like to connect, there is nothing stopping you from just calling to say hello. Don't mention that you saw he called because that could cause embarrassment to him.

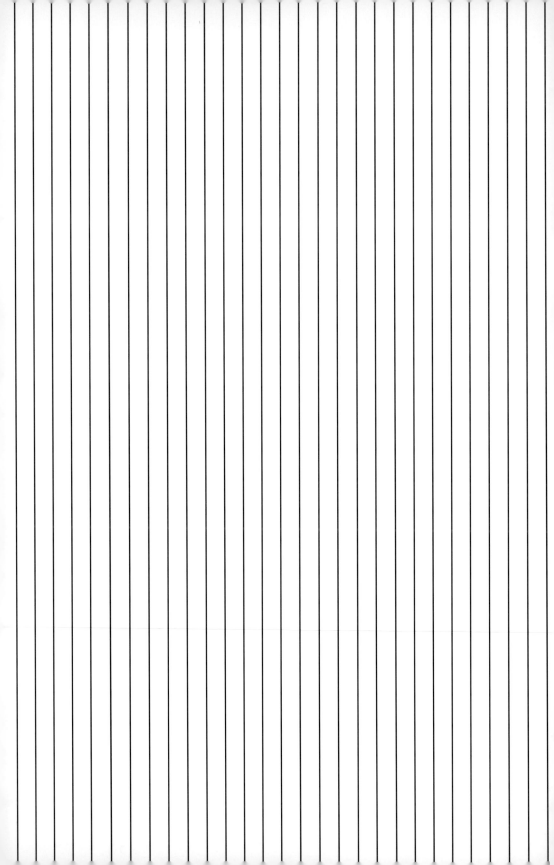

CHAPTER 6

MONEY

"Money makes the world go round." It is an important part of everyone's life. How we handle it is an everyday concern. How others handle their (and sometimes our) money influences our pleasant daily interactions. In this chapter, many grievances about money are shared and solutions are proposed about how to react to bad money decisions. Hopefully they will be helpful when dealing with people who view money differently than you do.

> "People who constantly brag about how much money they have [are very annoying]."
> —*Mark Rinaldi*

You hear bragging from those who feel flush at the moment and are trying to impress others by talking about something external rather than internal. ***The Solution:*** If you feel so inclined, when you are in a conversation with someone and his money situation comes up, kindly say, "Excuse me, but would you mind if we talk about something else? I'd really like to stay away from the topic of money, if that's all right with you." If he respects you, he will gladly change the topic. And if you are overhearing other wealthy people discussing their monetary situations, there is nothing wrong with listening and maybe learning how they earned their fortune. We could all use an inside track to wealth.

> "Broke people who beg for money should be spending their time looking for a job or improving their skills to get a job [I find this annoying]."
>
> —*Steven H. from Seattle, WA*

We judge others based upon our own value system. The way Steven would handle being down on his luck is exactly the way he expects others to act. When he doesn't see them reacting the same way, he complains that it offends his values. ***The Solution:*** Basically, we have no right to insist that others handle their lives the way we handle ours. At best, we can set an example or make suggestions, but if they are not heeded, we can just be kind and hope for their future success.

> "I'm annoyed when I see people trying to 'keep up with the Joneses' when they know they don't have any money."
>
> —*C. W Holmes*

The Solution: If this concern is for a friend, you could help his situation by complimenting him on the things he currently has which may not have cost a lot of money but show good taste. If you have nothing to compliment your friend on, then holding your tongue will be the best approach. We are all victims of society's pressures and some have a more difficult time of accepting their current predicament when they believe they should have everything others have. In my opinion, compassion is a more appropriate response than annoyance in this situation.

> "I become very upset with people who use the exact change toll lane and don't have their money ready"
>
> —*Charles P. from Miami, FL*

The Solution: Practice patience and understand that all people are not as organized as you.

"People who have no money when they get to the cash register at the store are really bothersome."

—*Many people's annoyance*

In this situation, if the shopper has already set out his or her purchases and now has to gather them up again, it wastes our time, which is annoying. *The Solution:* Remember that forgetting your wallet or purse can happen to anyone, on any given day, and should not be ridiculed but pitied. I definitely know what it feels like and I'm sure you do too.

"Whenever I get extra money something breaks! This annoys me greatly!"

—*George A. from Fairfax, VA*

I commiserate with you. I don't have an etiquette-based answer for this, but I do understand the frustration. The only thing I can really say is don't take it too hard—it's not bad luck or even bad karma. It's just life.

"Vending machines that take your money, especially when you don't have the time to find someone to retrieve [your money], are very frustrating."

—*Popular complaint across all socioeconomic lines*

It's true: No one wants to lose their money in a machine, especially when they are hungry. *The Solution:* Shrug it off. Just chalk it up as an unfortunate part of the day and don't let it get the best of you.

"It's annoying when I have a lack of money—especially when others seem to be spending big bucks."

—*Anonymous hundreds*

The Solution: Be happy for the people who are able to spend as they like. If the subject of money (or lack thereof) bothers you, don't engage in the conversation. Everyone's situation is different and you should respect that and also expect to be respected in return. We honestly don't know if the "big spenders" are spending money they have or don't have, and it is really none of our business.

> "People who have more money than I do [are] always expecting me to cover them."
>
> —*Pauly from Brookline, MA*

The Solution: Lament how tough times are and suggest less expensive recreational pursuits. Be ready to leave if they insist they can't pay their way. If you acquiesce once, they will try to take advantage again. You have all the power in this situation. Use it to say, "No!"

> "I hate it when people ask me how much money I make."
>
> —*George Matthews*

The Solution: There is a way to respond without giving away any real information. Tell them, "It is never enough" or "I am doing all right in that department." This way, you can feel relieved of having to state your salary and they will hopefully get the hint that they don't really need to know.

> "I'm frustrated when girlfriends ask how much I paid for a new item."
>
> —*Hannah from Beverly Hills, CA*

This is definitely tacky! ***The Solution:*** Try responding with, "I got a bargain!" or "It was a splurge that I treated myself to." Neither answer gives the price tag of the item and both answers will stop the interrogation immediately.

"Not having enough money to buy more gifts for all the people in my life who I truly appreciate [annoys me]."

—*Roger B. from Houston, TX*

The Solution: The best way to show your appreciation for others doesn't have to cost money, at least not much. Try writing them a letter—using your own words and sharing why they are important to you and why you cherish them. This gesture will be remembered long after whatever you might be able to afford from a store is forgotten.

"Standing in line at the grocery store behind a woman who can't find her money or checkbook or pen and then can't find her ID for the clerk is infuriating!"

—*Susan S. from Vermont*

Not wasting other people's time is a basic etiquette rule so losing valuable time due to someone else's disorganization is understandable. People who don't have money ready in the checkout line are a common source of complaint. If we are typically organized and have our credit card ready to swipe or cash in hand for the clerk, we expect others to be equally organized. *The Solution:* Rest assured that it won't take long to retrieve the payment and in the meantime, there are always those magazines to scan.

"I'm annoyed by politicians wasting our money."

—*Anonymous taxpayers*

Because this a common lament, it is often the topic of conversation. The old adage about staying away from politics in conversation applies. You have a credible peeve but the person with whom you are sharing it may be someone you don't know well and may have a different political viewpoint. You have a fifty-fifty chance of turning a perfectly pleasant conversation into a battleground if you engage. *The Solution:* Because there isn't a formula illustrating how to stop politicians from spending our well-earned dollars, a good way to change the subject would be to say, "None of us, including the government, have money to waste. However, this is a complicated subject that I am not interested in getting tangled up in right now. Let's talk politics when we know each other better. Have you read a good book lately?"

> "I become frustrated with people asking to borrow money when you know they have no intention of paying it back. It isn't just that they ask, but that I don't know how to say no to them. It is usually a relative or close friend and I don't want to seem stingy."
>
> —*Sandra P. from San Antonio, TX*

We allow ourselves to be taken advantage of in these types of situations because we want to be liked and we believe that if we say no, the other person won't like us. Nothing is further from the truth. ***The Solution:*** Just say no. Saying no when someone asks for money is easier if you say, "I like/love you and appreciate the situation that you are in. But our relationship is too important to me to let money become part of it. As a rule, I never lend. I'm sorry I can't help you."

If the borrower values your relationship then this should end the discussion. If he calls you stingy or something worse, then your relationship isn't as strong as you might like and perhaps you should take this as a clue.

> "People who 'borrow' money and 'forget' to pay it back are annoying."
>
> —*Many people's lament*

The Solution: If you are the lender, and you didn't have a written agreement to the terms of what was borrowed, for how long, and at what price, then the best you have is to simply ask for it to be returned. Sometimes, the borrower may have actually forgotten the obligation and only a gentle reminder is necessary to square accounts. However, there are borrowers who hope you forget to ask for the money back. In this case, you need to take the power position—explain that it has been a long time since you lent the money to him and that you need to establish some terms for repayment. Have something in writing ready to give to him and insist that you both agree to the terms at that moment. Don't put it off for another day's discussion—it is difficult enough to bring the subject up once. Most people will fume if they have to bring it up again to solve the problem.

"People who throw their money on the counter instead of just handing it to you infuriate me."

—*John Peterson (in retail) from Florida*

It seems so easy to nicely put the bills into the other person's hand. Having anything thrown at us denigrates the item being thrown and shows disrespect to the recipient. ***The Solution:*** If someone does this to you, just politely pick up the money and move on to the next customer. If you feel it necessary to challenge the person, be prepared for a scene—this person is probably already in a difficult mood and you'll get the brunt of it.

"I become annoyed when a cashier hands you your change and puts coins on top of the paper money."

—*Anonymous*

The Solution: Simply ask the clerk for the coins first, then put them away and take the paper money. It might take a few extra seconds, but the clerk will get the message and will hopefully continue to do the same thing for other potentially annoyed customers.

"Guys who have money but want you to pay your share are so annoying!"

—*Some irate women*

This is a social phenomenon that started in the 1960s and continued with the debate about the proposed Equal Rights Amendment. ***The Solution:*** Ladies, if this is a peeve of yours, there are plenty of old-fashioned, savvy men out there who wouldn't dream of allowing you to pay your own way. If you do find one of them, remember that the right thing to do is to reciprocate, maybe at your home with a home-cooked meal. Also, remember that whoever initiated the invitation to the event is the host and should pay for the guest.

> "People who do nothing but talk about money are annoying beyond belief."
>
> —*Anonymous*

In the United States as well as other parts of the world, money has long been considered a private subject. However, as humans, we search for commonalities to help us connect on a personal level. Money is a subject we all share. When the economy is low, there is more talk about it because we have been given "permission" by the media. It is the most common subject in the news reports and thus can become the most common subject we talk about with others. ***The Solution:*** If you don't want to engage in a conversation about money, politely tell the other person that it's a matter you'd rather not talk about at the moment. Suggest another topic.

> "People who spend serious money on equipment they never bother to learn to use are obnoxious."
>
> —*Anonymous*

Having this as a pet peeve is a reflection of having too much time to dwell on other people's spending choices. ***The Solution:*** Basically, it's none of your business and you should move on.

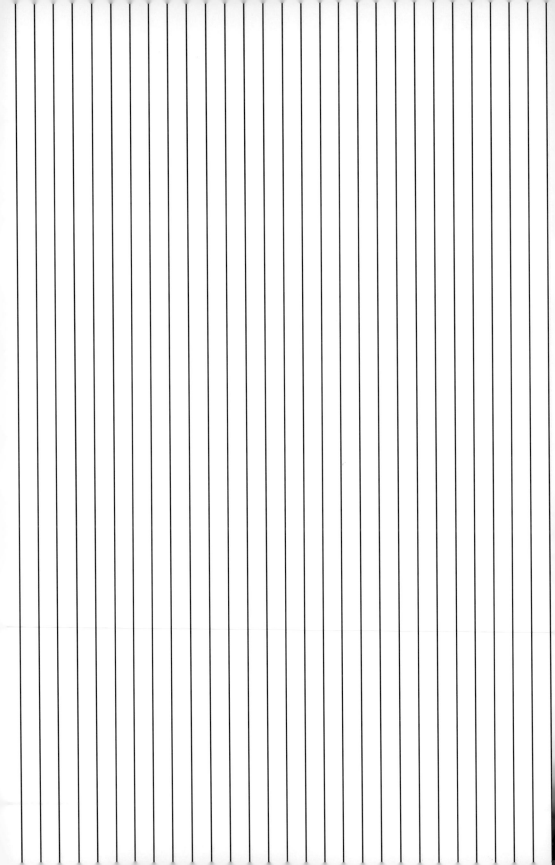

CHAPTER 7

DAILY LIVING

Every day, by virtue of just being out in the world, you open yourself up to other people and the possibility of encountering their most annoying behaviors. In our cars, we encounter road rage, cell phone talkers, makeup administrators, and worse. We walk on sidewalks and down hallways. We call for help from plumbers, electricians, cable installers, and the telephone company. Anytime we need help, we are vulnerable to the etiquette of whomever comes to our aid. Because the decline of proper etiquette abounds in today's society, we have to learn to cope with many frustrations.

Basic Manners

"One of my biggest pet peeves is rude people. Does it really hurt to say thank you, please, and you're welcome? And I include those people who say 'no problem' after you tell them thank you."

—*Desirée Greenlee-Powell*

In a world where the impression you leave on others matters more than ever, the simplest way to acknowledge the importance of positive interaction in our lives is to say please and thank you. ***The Solution:*** Be the model of good behavior. Always say "Please," Thank you," "Excuse me," and "You're welcome" and hopefully others around you will pick up on this nicety.

> "I don't hear these words [please and thank you] from anyone in my home but my social circle is courteous. My family believes that because
> they are family the rules of courtesy
> don't apply."
>
> —*G.H.K from Los Angeles*

Whether we are married to the person or are raising him, we are nonetheless entitled to be treated kindly. ***The Solution:*** If your family members forget the "magic words" on a regular basis, have a family meeting and discuss how you would appreciate it if they showed more courtesy around the house. In a sense, you'll be doing everyone a favor because by practicing good manners in our own homes, we are more likely to display those behaviors in public.

Interactions with People

Though I didn't receive many annoyances like this one, I still think it is appropriate to share. Caren of San Francisco offered her workplace frustration: "I work at an enormous facility with nice wide hallways and stairwells where one would not expect this to occur on account of the available space and, one presumes, well-mannered people. However, the wider hallways simply allow for a greater number of persons to walk abreast and create a moving wall. The worst offenders are doctors, often three- or even four-wide with stethoscopes swinging and coats flapping, forcing everyone aside. I have seen (I swear this is true!) a patient on crutches who had to quickstep and lean on a wall to dodge the oncoming tide. Sometimes, especially in a social setting such as leaving a restaurant, people are caught up in conversation and maneuvering coats, children, etc., and this is understandable. However, in most cases, there is no excuse. There may be an unconscious group- power thing going on, I don't know, but it annoys me to no end." When we witness a group of people engaging in selfish behavior at the expense of those who they are supposed to take care of, we judge their behavior more harshly. *The Solution:* A good response for Caren (and any of us ever put in this type of annoying situation) is for her to share her observation without commenting on how annoying it is. The fact that a patient was forced out of the way should open someone's eyes and change behavior in the hospital.

> "It irritates me to see people boarding trains or buses, or gaining entry anywhere (e.g., a building), oblivious to proper etiquette. Always let people exit a building or vehicle before entering. Not only is it courteous, but it is common sense."
>
> —*Jeanie Walker*

> "In the busy elevators at the hospital I work in, I have the most difficult time leaving the elevator because of all the people standing in the middle of the door and not giving me space to exit."
>
> —*Cissy*

The Solution: There is an etiquette rule that states that you let the people on the elevator off first and enter when it is empty. When it is time to exit, a quick "excuse me" is all you need to get out. Don't be afraid to make eye contact with the person or people who are blocking your exit route and ask them to kindly move so you can be on your way.

How Others Look

> "My biggest annoyance is with people who wear every
> piece of jewelry they own all at once. I've seen it on
> various people in all walks of life. They need to show
> the world that they have valuables, so they wear it all,
> sometimes two rings on each finger. Coworkers are
> distracted by the 'bling' and less able to focus on
> the person and what he or she is saying to them."
>
> —*Pauldine France*

We all have our personal standards about what looks good to us and what looks overdone. Though wearing an abundance of jewelry is considered poor etiquette in the business world, it also distracts from the looks and charm of the person when in a social situation. Jewelry's purpose is to enhance the wearer's appearance—not to be the only thing others see. When we are with others, our goal is to interact with them, making them feel comfortable and respected. ***The Solution:*** Though you may feel annoyed by people all "blinged out," unless you really know the person and feel comfortable telling her that her excessive jewelry wearing is gaudy, just shrug it off and tell yourself that it's not worth getting annoyed over.

> "People looking dirty, shabby, and unkempt (especially
> unpolished shoes) along with cluttered rooms and
> workspaces are my biggest annoyances."
>
> —*Barbara Aragon from the Philippines*

The Solution: If the person with the questionable hygiene and clothes is someone close to you, take him aside and tell him that you are concerned with his unkemptness. If you are in a leadership position, explain the negative effect his appearance has on his success in business. Offer to help if you can suggest places close by where he can polish his shoes, for instance. But you cannot control everyone's appearance or behavior and sometimes you just need to look the other way and move on.

Youthful Fashion Statements

Boys who follow the trend of wearing jeans with crotches that hang to their knees, exposing their underwear, have gotten under the skin of lawmakers in many communities. "Indecent exposure" is their explanation.

Marcus of Illinois shared a funny observation: "It is an absolute riot to watch them run with their pants down around their knees. My boys and I have watched it a few times. One hand swinging, the other trying to hold their pants up so they can run. It's penguin-like, yes indeed."

For reasons unknown to those of us who are not hip-hop aficionados, this slovenly fashion statement for boys and young men is rampant. I can't understand why anyone would want others to know the color and style of his underwear. Sometimes common sense should prevail. If this is an annoyance of yours, I suggest that you look the other way. If the young man is someone you know and have a good relationship with, you can ask him why he chooses to wear

---

Personal Habits

As we go through our days, we notice the little things that people do that shouldn't bother us but for whatever reason, they drive us nuts. A few that you shared are:
- Licking fingers to turn a page—ignore them
- Cutting fingernails in the office or in the car—ask them to do this in private
- When I hear someone repeatedly clicking a pen or tapping a pencil on the table while talking to me, I ask them to stop.

his pants so low. Perhaps he has an interesting reason. In fact, this fashion has been traced to inmates' uniforms in prison—the sagging pants are a result of prisoners not being able to wear belts. However, if there is no good reason for the underwear display, you can suggest that when he's out and about, it would be better for him to put on a belt and pull up his pants a little bit—just for the sake of decency.

Chewing Gum and Spitting

> "People who chew gum in public—public being anywhere there is another person, outside of your own personal living quarters—are ugly."
>
> —*Anonymous anti-gum chewers*

The Solution: This is another instance where you cannot control the actions of others. Though public gum chewing may be annoying to you, there is no special "rule" against it and, just like the person walking their dog down the street or the person smoking outside, it is a personal choice and one we shouldn't let get the better of us. However, chewing gum never makes anyone look attractive.

> "Spitting on sidewalks and parking lots is an omnipresent act that is totally disgusting! If one needs to get rid of phlegm use a tissue or at least be considerate enough to eject into a flower bed or trash receptacle. Better yet, blow your nose before it settles in your throat or simply swallow!"
>
> —*Leslie McHugh*

The Solution: Again, do you really think it possible to control the actions of others? If the spitter is someone you know, by all means, tell the offender it is gross and to blow his nose. Otherwise, just avert your eyes and don't pay attention to the public spitters. And watch your step!

"The sound of someone clearing their throat and
then spitting turns my stomach."

—*Rita Harman*

The Solution: Ignore it and chalk it up to narcissism.

Touching

"I think it's obnoxious when people pick things off of your
clothes while they are talking with you, without your
permission."

—*Anonymous*

The Solution: Tell the person "thanks" but that the next time you
have lint on your clothes, he should just tell you and not go grab-
bing for it himself. It is important to make your boundaries known to
others.

"It's very annoying to have someone 'fix' a
label that is showing on your shirt without asking
you if they may do so."

—*Anonymous*

The Solution: I consider this to be a kindness when someone wants
me to look more pulled together. However, if you don't share my
opinion, when someone does this for you, just say "thanks" and then
let him know that if he sees the label up the next time, to just tell you
to fix it yourself. You appreciate the concern but just don't like other
people touching your clothing.

Guests in Your Home

> "I hate it when friends or other guests in my home insist on getting a tour. I do not know of anything more stressing for a homeowner. How rude!"
>
> —*Alexa from Chicago*

The Solution: Just say no. If your home isn't up to showcase status at the moment, you should tell the guest that you appreciate his interest but you would prefer not to give tours today; perhaps another time. But understand that the guest's insistence comes from curiosity about how you have decorated and the desire to learn more about you by seeing how your private life is led. These are understandable feelings but you, the host, have the power to say "Thank you for your interest but no." You should never be made to feel uncomfortable in your own home.

When giving a recent dinner party, Jessica of Rhode Island was put in a difficult etiquette position when one of her guests who had responded for just herself brought along a friend. Jessica had planned the dinner meticulously and lives in a rather small apartment with limited space for guests. There just wasn't room for the friend and the other expected guests, and she hadn't planned on enough food for an extra guest. She allowed the two of them in, but it ruined the flow and comfort of the evening for not just Jessica but also the other guests who were now crowded. ***The Solution:*** There is a proper way to handle this situation and it depends upon the host's planning and circumstances. If you have the space to easily set another place, that would be ideal. If you didn't plan enough food for one extra, then give yourself a much smaller portion and allow your guests what you had already planned for. (I always plan for one extra, just in case.) If there is not enough room at the table for all, some quick rearranging to make the dinner a buffet may solve the problem. You may have to sit on the floor but after all, you are the host. Your guests' comfort comes first.

If accommodating an unexpected guest is impossible, the proper thing is to take the person who you originally invited to a private space out of earshot of their tag-along and explain that you were happily anticipating his coming, but alone as he had told you when he replied. Say, "Because of space restrictions, there isn't going to be enough space for one more so could we make another date to have dinner in the near future?" You know they understand the situation they have put you in. Say you are sorry but it just won't work tonight. If you have to say this to someone, don't accept his hostess gift if he brought one. Try to keep him from interacting with your other guests or things will become even more awkward. Most importantly, don't feel guilty that you could not accommodate the extra guest—it's your friend's fault for imposing the extra person on your well-planned evening. If you still feel guilty, call the guest the next day and explain again why you could not include an extra person. Hopefully that will be the last time your guest springs an unexpected person on an unsuspecting host.

> "I entertain at my home whenever I can and my guests always bring wine as a hostess gift. I hardly ever like their taste in wine but they insist I open it for serving that night."
>
> —*Rita from Washington*

The hostess gift is a problem for many guests. Guests have heard from their friends that wine is the perfect choice so they bring wine. They also feel that they should contribute in some way to the festivity of the evening beyond their sparkling personality so they want you to open their wine. Both assumptions are incorrect and frustrate many hosts and hostesses. ***The Solution:*** When you are the guest, model the right way to give a gift by bringing something relevant to entertaining but not edible or drinkable If you are the host and do receive wine, thank the giver and state that it would be wonderful to try at a later time and that you hope he likes the wine you are serving this evening. This will indicate that it will not be opened at that time.

"I'm frustrated when I have people in my home who break something and then either don't own up to it and offer to replace whatever it was, or who hide the broken item for me to find sometime later."

—*Mary from Kansas City, KS*

Well, it happens. Things get broken unexpectedly and accidentally. It is a basic etiquette rule that when you invite someone into your home and something gets broken, it is just the cost of entertaining. ***The Solution:*** You really can't ask someone to replace what was broken. However, if you have classy klutzes in your circle of friends and they break something, it is totally up to you whether you want to accept the offer to replace the shattered item.

Driving

Key Complaints

Being cut off in traffic

Not using a turn signal

Putting on makeup or shaving while driving

Reading a newspaper or book while driving

Driving slowly in the left lane

Tailgating

Obscene gestures from other driver

Road rage is a common and disturbing trend in society, in all countries where there are cars and drivers. So many drivers believe that when they are inside of a car, even one with six or more windows, they are invisible. When we feel invisible, we feel freer to act out, believing others won't react. Many have started acting out their anger behind the wheel which is why road rage is so scary. When drivers are victims of being cut off, tailgated, or slowed down by a vehicle in front of them, some may lose their cool and resort to retaliation through violence. The key point to keep in mind while driving is that it is not a competition. It is a method of getting from here to there and we should definitely not let our annoyance get the best of our better judgment while operating a motor vehicle.

> "In California while driving on the freeway many slow drivers move to the left lane oblivious of the flow of traffic. They never move over! I have seen this only in California. The two lanes to the right go faster (with the flow of traffic) than the left lane. This makes me think such a person wants to demonstrate their control issues [and annoy me]."
>
> —*Sandy Jolley*

I have seen this in almost every state that I have driven in, and I agree that it is a control issue. Instead of getting out of someone's way, the slow driver is saying, "I know the speed limit and I am going to obey the law no matter what. If you really want to advance past me, go around me any way you can, but I am holding my ground." **The Solution:** Because you cannot really control at what speed someone else is comfortable driving, but you'd like to use the left lane to pass, try flashing your bright lights to signal the driver ahead of you to move over to the right lane. If that does not work, back off from the driver, give him adequate space, and just accept the fact that you might be behind this car for a while.

> "Drivers who go through residential neighborhoods with their radios up full blast and cars rocking are extremely annoying."
>
> —*Anonymous*

Drivers who do this are not usually of a mind to listen to your complaint. ***The Solution:*** Just smile and drive on. If you are in your house, busy yourself with something else or turn up the TV volume. They will be gone shortly.

> "I'm annoyed with people who don't stop at stop signs."
>
> *—Various drivers*

There ought to be a law! Oh, yes—there is. ***The Solution:*** If you can, take down the license plate of the car and call it into the local police station.

> "Drivers who drive without lights in the rain and
> at night are bothersome and hard to see."
>
> *—Many annoyed people*

Perhaps these offenders really don't know what they are doing. ***The Solution:*** Flash your lights at them a couple of times to remind them. This usually happens when they start their trip in a well-lit area and the lights are not yet needed. It is a kindness to everyone on the road to let them know.

> "It's terribly annoying to see trash or a lit cigarette being
> thrown out of a car."
>
> *—Anonymous*

There are laws in almost all states against littering. ***The Solution:*** I recommend taking down the license plate number and reporting it to the local police station.

> "People who change lanes without looking to see if there
> is a car next to them are dangerous and annoying."
>
> *—Various drivers*

The Solution: Situations like this one call for your best defensive driving. Assume at all times that the other driver will do something stupid. Be ready to handle it without incident. Anticipate the problem. Be smart—not annoyed. Intelligence will help you stay safe in the end.

> "Old people who drive annoy me."
>
> *—Common complaint*

Only family members can stop an elderly person from driving if he is impaired. *The Solution:* We do have the power to keep out of his way. Give some extra room—his reaction time to situations is bound to be slower than yours.

An Aside

The most prevalent complaint people have is about drivers who talk on their cell phones. More than seventy-five percent of my submitters claimed this as their number one annoyance. When I am driving, it appears that every time there is a near miss or accident, the driver was talking or texting on the phone. When you see someone driving with a cell phone in plain view, be wary and keep your distance. Furthermore, you can't stop someone from personal grooming while he is driving but keep your disgust to yourself. Shaking your head and gesturing towards him can rile up anger and frustration, resulting in road rage. If kids are in the car with me, I tend to say, "Yes, kids, you can look to see what I am talking about," to teach them what not to do while driving. Then when the teaching moment is over, keep as far away from the driver as possible.

Random Annoyance About Driving

> "I hate driving by a pig farm when the top is down
> and it's ninety-five degrees."
>
> —*Conrad Williams*

Well, Conrad—I can just smell it! Hopefully there isn't much traffic and you can drive by quickly (of course keep to the speed limit).

The Traveling Public

Key Complaints (about our traveling companions)

Talk too much

Don't talk at all

Spread out their things during a flight

Constantly get up and climb over people

Let their children cry too much

Let their children stare at someone from the back of the seat in front of him

Let their children kick someone's seat

Recline their seats too far back

Grab the back of someone's seat when moving around

Have too much luggage/carry-on stuff

Spill things

Use someone's space without asking permission

Use someone else's armrests

Constantly buzz the attendants

Barf

Sing along with their iPod

How to Model Appropriate Driving Behavior

- We have control over only ourselves when driving, and we can make our car trips more pleasant by keeping our attitude positive.
- Be cautious in case the other driver does something discourteous or aggressive.
- Be courteous. Set the example of how it should be done.
- Signal when you change or merge lanes.
- Use your horn rarely—only if you feel threatened.
- Adopt the "be my guest" attitude. If another driver and you see the same parking space, let him have it. If another driver wants to get in front of you, say, "Be my guest."
- Most important, if another driver does something nice for you, acknowledge the gesture with a wave of your hand in your rearview mirror. When we are appreciated for the nice things we do, we tend to repeat the behavior.

A Few Things to Remember While Traveling

- Few like to sit squished in a small space they can't get out of, for hours on end, next to people they don't know.
- There are ways of handling the annoyances listed earlier that don't involve staying home.
- It is important to know that good etiquette comes from asking permission rather than making demands of other people.

It is not difficult to understand why airline travel is so hard. It isn't the airplane itself or the fact that people's comfort and self-confidence diminishes in proportion to the distance they are from their homes. No, the hardest part of travel is giving the other travelers a break. More people informed that their annoyance with other travelers was their main problem while away from home.

When the family traveling with children seems to be letting the kids run loose, instead of fuming, help. Say hello to the mother or father, introduce yourself (people always react more kindly to someone whose name they know), explain that you understand how difficult it must be for the children to be stuck on the plane for so long (in kids' eyes, ten minutes can be forever), how restless they must be, and ask if you can help. Most likely the kids are bored rather than obnoxious by nature and parents sometimes just give up the fight. Ask permission of the parents to talk to the child. Get the parent on your side with respect and compassion. Experience bears out that the parents will be more proactive in keeping little Johnny or Sally from bothering the nice man (or lady).

What if the person sitting next to you starts talking the moment he sits down and won't stop? First of all, understand that he is not trying to ruin your flight. He just hasn't been informed by you of what your expectations and wishes are. Try this: Smile, introduce yourself, and validate them. React to something they say—have a three-minute conversation if you can. Then tell him, "I am glad to have met you. I am finally able to read this book I have been looking forward to and know you won't mind leaving me to do so." Or "I plan to use my time on this flight to catch up on all the paperwork I brought with me. You would be doing me a great favor if we didn't talk for a while so I can concentrate." The point is that you ask for permission to help accomplish what you want on the flight. Getting his cooperation for the nap you plan to take will assure you a quiet rest.

Getting the pleasant outcome that you want from a flight is as easy as asking for it. Unfortunately, it is more common for people to "stew" in their indignation at someone's "rude" behavior. The next time the passenger in front of you reclines his seat all the way into your lap, introduce yourself, validate, and request. It could sound like this: "Excuse me. Hello, I am Cynthia Lett and I know how uncomfortable the seats can be but would you mind raising your seat a bit so I can have some room to cross my legs? I would really appreciate it." We are more likely to comply with someone's request if it is offered in a calm, kind manner. We are much less likely to care what the other person wants if he demands that we do what he wants.

If you would like to talk during a flight, the first thing to do is assess your seatmate's body language. Did he smile at you as you sat down? Is he still smiling? Does he look approachable? If you see positive responses to these questions you have a good chance for a conversation. First, introduce yourself. We feel more connected to someone if we know his name and maybe a little about him. You could add if you are coming from or going home. If this is your first trip to the destination, you might mention that. Anything you mention will help start the conversation. If you noticed he had beautiful luggage, compliment him on it. If his child is particularly well behaved, that would be good to mention as well. Ask his opinion about something that you have shared—the wait in the airport, the lateness of the flight, the kindness of the crew in handling the delay. If you agree with your seatmate's opinion state that you have that in common. If you don't, you should try to change the subject. Seat conversation is small talk so keep it light. But . . . if you see his arms folded across his chest—in essence putting up a wall—get the signal, say hello, introduce yourself, and wish him a pleasant flight. Then, stop talking. If he changes his mind about conversation, they will make the overture.

Please keep in mind that travel is difficult for most of us and we all need the kindness of others to make the experience tolerable if not pleasant. Be kind and patient with others who are squished into seats near you. They just need to be reminded that you are friendly and on their side—not an adversary they cannot escape.

Punctuality

One of the basics of good etiquette is not to waste other people's time. Lack of punctuality is just that—wasting others' time. We resent not only the time lost but the mood it puts us in after we have been required to wait for someone. No one likes to wait for others because one feels it shows a lack of respect for his time. If you know that someone is chronically late and you choose to schedule a meeting with him, plan accordingly. Perhaps give him a meeting time that is fifteen minutes earlier than you really want him there. Or, plan on something to keep you busy while you wait for him to show up. Or, better yet, tell him what he will miss if he arrives after your indicated time. Perhaps some people only need an incentive to get where they agree to be on time. Though keeping a sense of humor would help resolve the resentment, it only works if you have something to occupy yourself while you are waiting. With cell phones today offering multiple forms of entertainment and utility, perhaps this could be a good distraction. Also a book, magazine, or article could come in handy. If we accomplish something while waiting for someone else, we won't harbor resentment for the latecomer and their lack of consideration.

> "I resent waiting at a restaurant for people who never show and don't call to cancel!"
>
> —*Sara Torrance from Maryland*

This is totally understandable! ***The Solution:*** The rule for waiting for someone is after fifteen minutes call him and see if something has happened. If you cannot reach him and you check with the manager to see if he called, you would be right to leave a written note with the manager or front desk stating that you are sorry you could not connect and that he should call to reschedule. Likewise, if you invite someone to a meal at your home and he is more than fifteen minutes late, you should call him to check on his arrival. If you hear nothing by twenty minutes after his expected arrival time, you would be correct to start eating with the other guests or even by yourself.

> "People showing up late for work is annoying."
>
> —*Complaint among many coworkers*

When we depend on others to be there to do work which impacts our work, it can lead to problems. ***The Solution:*** If you are in a position of authority, call the person into your office (privately) and say that his behavior is unacceptable and that work begins promptly at the designated time. If you are a coworker and observe someone's tardiness, you could just ignore it (again, you cannot necessarily control the behaviors of others) or you could ask your coworker why he has trouble coming to work on time. Perhaps he has a legitimate excuse and then you have no legitimate annoyance.

"Latecomers in a theater are my biggest pet peeve."

—*Rochelle B. from London*

When you are settled into your seat watching a performance, the latecomer not only disrupts you as they pass in front of you, but also the guests behind you. ***The Solution:*** This is one of those scenarios when saying something might make an even bigger scene. If the person comes in and sits down right away, then just forget about it and enjoy the show. Either way, latecomers should not ruin your movie-watching experience—and don't let them!

"I'm annoyed with people who think they know what a late person is thinking (e.g. 'My time is more important than yours') but many times it's not true. Sometimes you are just dealing with unplanned interruptions that throw your schedule off. Then, when you try to keep your appointments, you end up arriving late. Why can't people understand that?"

—*Jocelyne D. from North Dakota*

The Solution: Calmly explain your situation and apologize for being late. And if you know that you have a good excuse for being late, don't worry so much about what others think.

"Mom makes me late for school. I'm just a kid and have no control over when my mom is ready to leave in the morning. I'm always ready on time so I have to wait. This is my pet peeve."

—*Mickie Williams from Arkansas*

I share this frustration because my mother seemed to be late for everything in her life, especially taking and picking me up to go places. If it was something important such as school, I made certain that the tardiness was not blamed on me because I lacked control of the situation. There are situations that cannot be fixed unless the adult realizes what they are doing and decides to change his behavior. ***The Solution:*** I suggest soliciting the help of another adult close to the offender to convey the problem and the child's concerns.

> "People who are always late and then tell you that you're too uptight because you're not are annoying."

> "People who think it's cool to be 'fashionably late' for everything are frustrating."

> —*Anonymous annoyances*

Being fashionably late is a misnomer. It is never fashionable to be late. It is just rude. There is a standard of what constitutes "lateness" to an event, however. If the occasion takes place at someone's home, don't be exactly on time and for heavens sake, don't be early unless specifically asked to be by the host. Entertaining is stressful enough without your host having to worry about entertaining you before everything is ready. Arriving exactly at 7 pm for a 7 pm cocktail hour doesn't allow the host a minute to breathe. You would be kinder to arrive three or four minutes after 7 pm. ***The Solution:*** Know what the rules are for being "appropriately" late and don't be so eager to judge those running a little behind schedule. If you are the host and a guest breaks these rules, then you have grounds for sharing your disappointment or anticipating an apology upon their arrival.

Procrastination

"I'm frustrated with people who procrastinate or who live by the mantra 'I'll do this later.'"

> —*Anonymous*

The Solution: How we handle others' putting off what needs to be done is determined by our priorities, not theirs. If it is really important to you to have them handle something immediately, don't just expect them to, explain to them why it is important and perhaps offer your assistance.

The TV

Key Complaints (About Watching TV)

All the Christmas shopping commercials before

Thanksgiving

People who take reality TV seriously

New programs that inform about TV shows

People talking during a TV show

People who talk to the TV as if the TV is going to respond

Bad grammar used by actors and newscasters—shouldn't

they be role models?

Stupid commercials

TV ads—too many, too stupid, too explicit

The TV that is left on all day when no one is watching

"I can't stand how the TV networks get together to synchronize their commercials so I can't flip from the show I am watching to another when a commercial is on. They all go to commercial at the same time."

—*Maggie S. from New Hampshire*

Though this certainly is annoying for the average TV viewer, there is really not much you can do about it. So, if you are annoyed with commercials, perhaps getting a DVR would help eliminate some of these frustrations. Then you can record your favorite show (and skip the commercials when you eventually watch it) and browse other channels during regular airtime.

Handicap Parking Spaces

"It's annoying when others use the designated handicap spaces and don't qualify for the convenience."

—Anonymous handicapped drivers

As someone who has unfortunately earned my handicapped car plates and placard with multiple surgeries and residual physical difficulties, I agree with this annoyance. Just because there are no other spaces close to the store and you just have to run in for a quick moment, this doesn't qualify you to read the future and know that a qualified owner of a handicap license plate won't be coming into the parking lot while you are there. We don't mind it if others who share our plight are there first, but when someone who is able-bodied intrudes, we do get upset. ***The Solution:*** You can go into the store or building and complain to the owner. Or, you can call the local police and report the incident. At times, I have asked the offender if perhaps he didn't notice the handicapped sign and took the space when someone who truly needed it was left to walk a much greater distance.

Soliciting

"[I'm fed up with] door-to-door solicitors who try to intimidate you into believing their religion, favorite nonprofit, or list of magazines you must buy to help them go on a trip is something you need to hear about or contribute to. People are not being brave enough to say 'No thanks, I don't want the pamphlet.' Instead they complain about being bullied into accepting whatever was being hawked."

—*Harry from Bethesda, MD*

The Solution: We have all the power when we are in our home and to allow a stranger to take the power from you for the sake of "being nice" and then complaining about it to others shows your inability to stand up for yourself. You can, at any time, refuse to open the door to a stranger. If you do open the door, you also have the right to kindly say, "Thanks for stopping by but I don't have the time or the interest in what you are selling/saying. I wish you a nice day and I need to go now." And shut the door. Simple as that.

Pets

"Why do pet owners assume that I am ok with their dogs jumping on me when I come in the front door, their cats rubbing up against my pant legs (usually black material), or any combination of the above mentioned animals seating themselves next to me on the sofa or on top of my feet? I like animals and I am glad that pets are such an important part of people's lives, but don't assume I want your pets all over me. Pet owners . . . please ask first if I mind . . . because I do. This is especially annoying when I visit a client's home and the pet has to become part of the conversation."

—*Carol from New Mexico*

The Solution: If you know the person whose home you are going to and you don't want his pet to invade your space, tell him ahead of time (politely, of course). If you arrive at someone's home who unexpectedly has a pet, be nice but ask if he would mind removing the pet to another part of the house while you talk with him. Most pet owners will oblige, especially if you have an allergy or a fear of animals.

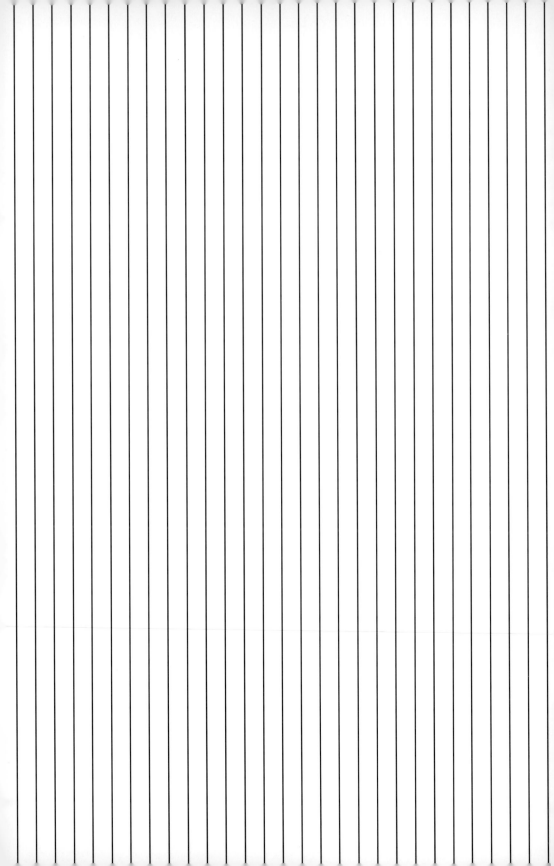

CHAPTER 8

COMMUNICATION

The greatest joy in many lives is personal interaction with others. We receive validation as to whether we are important or not from two-way communication. This chapter deals with conversation and language. But our communication is not only the words we say (they actually are only ten percent of our message), or the tone of voice we use (only thirty percent of our message), but our body language. A common annoyance is the gap between what people "say" and what they express nonverbally. Our body language, comprised of our facial expressions, position of our hands, feet, and arms, and our posture, gives meaning to the words that we use.

The majority of the complaints I received were about using language. Cursing and not speaking English well were by far the worst offensces. Though English is the most commonly spoken language in the world, it certainly is not the only one. If we know that someone is a native speaker of another language, we do tend to give them a pass at proper grammar and syntax. For the purpose of this volume, the complaints received were generally about the English language from native speakers.

New Verbiage

"The saying 'my bad' drives me nuts!"

—*Anonymous*

It started in Hollywood and on television and because it is a short-cut to real conversation—it caught on too well. It sounds silly, stupid, and juvenile to half of my contributors. What was wrong with saying, "That was my fault?" ***The Solution:*** If this is really bothersome to you and you know a person who uses this phrase regularly, just nicely ask him to try to refrain from using "my bad" around you—just tell him it irks you but that it's not a reflection of how you feel about him in general. People typically understand that there are just certain things that annoy us and they will most likely try to comply with your request.

"I don't appreciate the 'whatever' comeback. It's incredibly annoying"

—*Various irked individuals*

The use of the word "whatever" is rampant in the language of everyone. If I had said "whatever" to my parents, to a teacher, or even to the parents of a friend, I would have been branded as impudent and rude and probably wouldn't have had dinner that night. It is still considered rude to those of us over a certain age (if you think it is rude, then you are definitely of that age) but the ones who say it don't understand why. For the younger generation, it is just easier than trying to make a point using real words and coherent thoughts. The problem here is that we have let it get to this point without insisting on getting a proper response from the one saying it.

The Solution: If you know the person who says "whatever," be brave and tell the person that you think this phrase is inappropriate and suggest they stop using it. If you are a parent, you can set a rule for your children and establish some disciplinary action if the word is used inappropriately (especially when you've asked them to do something or change some behavior).

> "I'm frustrated when someone talks to you without giving you a chance to speak and when you try, they get mad."
>
> —*Paul from Virginia*

This is a good example of a one-sided conversation and few of us enjoy these. ***The Solution:*** If your conversation is turning out like this, it would be best to smile and say, "It was nice talking with you. Maybe we can continue our conversation another time." There are people who just like to hear themselves talk and having someone in front of them to talk with is more socially acceptable than talking to themselves and the air around them.

Greetings

Handshakes

How we initially greet someone in America is both a tactile and visual encounter. We extend out hand, feel the handshake, and see the expression of pleasure (a smile, bright eyes) on the person's face we are greeting.

Quite a few professionals understand that the handshake is the foundation of a relationship. Pauline France of Miami, Florida, summed it up for many when she described her assessment of one kind of bad handshake: She calls them "noodles." She explains that, "[A limp handshake] tells me that the person is either intimidated by the situation, lacks confidence, or simply doesn't know any better and assumes that it is 'ladylike.'" Because greetings are an important part of the first impression we leave on others, it is imperative that we pay attention to the way we shake hands.

The "No-no" Handshakes

1. The "wet noodle" or "limp fish." This handshake, as evidenced above, is weak and unassertive.
2. The "bone crusher." This handshake is when one person squeezes so hard they are apt to crush the bones of the other person's hand.
3. The "pumper." This handshake comes from an intense up-and-down pumping of the whole arm by one person. The recipient feels as if their arm will be yanked off.
4. The two-handed handshake. This handshake shows a dominance of one person over the other ("I have two hands and you only have one").

"When a principal executive who is in a receiving line gives no eye contact when they are shaking your hand but just gives you the limp fish handshake while pushing you along, is extremely annoying. It is as if saying, 'Now move on, let's get this over with. You have no importance to me.' This person displays no warmth or sincerity and you can feel that it is not from the heart, but an unwanted formality that they must participate in."

—*Alona Collins from Atlanta, GA*

This is a great example that shows the importance of eye contact in conveying the feeling that the other person wants to connect with you in an exchange. *The Solution:* No matter what, always reciprocate with a strong, firm handshake. Perhaps your solid grip will snap him out of his self-indulgent daze and you'll get the recognition you hope for. Also, if you happen to know the exec's name, use it when you shake his hand and see if his eyes don't suddenly shoot over to meet yours.

"I greatly dislike the knuckle bangers."

—*Anonymous*

It seems that Hollywood has started a new method of greeting each other—banging knuckles instead of shaking hands. The argument for this is that it is germ-phobic friendly. The argument against it is that it is unfriendly and looks like it will hurt you. Personally, I think it looks silly and defeats the purpose of a friendly greeting. **The Solution:** If someone comes up to me with his fist out and wants to hit my fist as a hello, I allow it because I don't know if they are germ phobic or just trying to keep up with Hollywood's interpretation of friendly. My judgment of that person suffers, nevertheless.

Kissing

> "'Air kissing' looks so ridiculous! It is embarrassing to watch and I hate it when a woman does it to me."
>
> —*Paul P. from Denver, CO*

It does look insincere but it started in Hollywood so we can understand that. Its purpose is to get close enough to the person you are greeting to look like you want to kiss him hello or goodbye but not close enough to smear your makeup or have her feel your whiskers. **The Solution:** If you are annoyed by having to involve yourself in this act, you could give a quick hug or go along with it this once. And if you don't like having women blowing kisses to you, just tell them that you would rather have a real kiss or no kiss—see what happens then (but only do this with a woman you really know well).

Bonus: But what about the proper etiquette regarding cheek or mouth kissing? If you are meeting your spouse in a business situation, a kiss on the cheek is appropriate. On-the-mouth kissing is never considered appropriate in business settings—it's too intimate. How about when you see someone you used to work with and had a close relationship with once upon a time? Keep it at a handshake. The reason why kissing and hugging are not correct isn't about what the two engaging in the greeting are feeling. It is the impression the two are giving to the watchers close by. They are thinking to themselves, "What is their relationship really?" "Why doesn't he greet me like that?" "What does she see in him that I don't have?" All of these reactions are not about business but about the way others feel about not being treated to the same intimacy that the person being kissed or hugged is. Hugging has the same connotations. It is more intimate than shaking hands, so those who are watching make assumptions that may or may not be true about the relationship the two people really share. Even when someone at work comes at you with arms wide open and the intent to hug, smile and put out your hand to shake and you will be taken more seriously.

Hey, Dude!

> "I hate it when people call me 'dude.'"
>
> —*Laura from New Hampshire*

This slang term is fine with close friends who use it affectionately, but most of the times I hear it, it is not by someone trying to be sweet. Instead, it is a shortcut to asking what someone's name is and showing he cares enough about the person to think knowing his name is important. ***The Solution:*** If someone you don't know comes up and calls you "Dude," instead of becoming annoyed, give him a smile and say, "I'm sorry. My name is Cynthia. I don't know any 'Dudes' around here." I'm sure you'll get a chuckle and then the person will know to call you by name.

Cursing

Many years ago there was a sign in a barber shop in Huntingburg, Indiana, that read: PROFANITY IS THE EFFORT OF A FEEBLE MIND TO EXPRESS ITSELF FORCIBLY. I understand that it kept the patrons of the shop from expressing themselves with curse words. Cursing has always been part of language but when individuals choose swear words over intelligent vernacular, the meaning of what they are saying deteriorates and so does any respect for the ones with whom they are conversing.

"I am bothered by cursing in public, especially when
children are around. It is rude and disrespectful. Show a
little class and show our youth how to respect themselves
and those around them."

—*Sherri Boover*

Many of us let loose with a curse word or two if something surprising or painful happens to us. ***The Solution:*** It's hard when we cannot control the actions of others—especially when those bad behaviors really irk us. If you see children present or even if you feel strong enough to do so, you can say to the swearer, "Excuse me but would you mind taking your conversation away from me? I don't think your language is appropriate for the people/children sitting around you." You may get a snotty remark, but at least you tried to avert the negative behavior.

"People who cuss in front of young kids
[are my annoyance]"

—*Martin L.*

I concur. If society is going to progress, we need to allow our children to grow up with as little negativity and as much proper language as possible. ***The Solution:*** Tell the person that there are young kids around and that you believe he should either find a different way of speaking or move elsewhere. It can't hurt to speak up about it, now can it?

All in all, cursing is sometimes humorous, but sometimes abusive. It can help vent anger, or provoke it. It can relieve stress, or cause it. It can be clever and flirtatious, or sexist and intimidating. Consequently, be aware of when and where you swear. Control it, tame it, time it. Or, to be on the safe side, stop using it altogether.

Cursing and Business

Business publications report an increase in profanity in the workplace and that cursing is considered unprofessional and offensive to many workers. Though the perpetrator may not always mean harm, it often creates a negative or hostile environment, sometimes leading to sexual harassment and violence. An article that was published by the Web site OnRec.com on April 4, 2008, stated that a foul mouth takes the top two spots in top ten office offenses. The world-renowned chef and restaurateur Gordon Ramsay enforces a no-swearing rule in his restaurants, and a report from TheLadders.co.uk reveals that one in ten UK bosses have fired an employee for swearing at work, and over seventeen percent have shown employees the door for bad manners such as lunchtime drinking, personal calls, and gossiping. The poll of more than 1,000 bosses reveals that forty-seven percent of bosses would fire for bad language. Not surprisingly, ninety-six percent of senior managers said that they would find a foul-mouthed colleague unacceptable to work alongside in the office.

Talking in Quiet Spaces

> "I find it extremely disturbing when people engage
> in detailed conversation (whether whispered or not)
> during a lecture or seminar. Not only is it rude to the
> featured speaker(s) but also inconsiderate to listeners.
> Such people should present their own seminars
> instead of attending those of others!"
>
> —*G.M.*

As a professional speaker, there are audiences I have been in front of that contain a constant talker. It is my job to control the room so it is my job to stop the talking. But it has to be done in a respectful manner. *The Solution:* If you are giving the lecture, you could say, "Excuse me. [Mr. Talker], what is your opinion on what I just said?" That question will bring the offender back into the group and highlight his indiscretion without stating out loud how rude he has been to me and those around him. Understand that talkers in inappropriate situations are usually bored with what is being discussed. If you bring the chatter into it personally, he stops. If you are a fellow audience member who is annoyed by this constant chatter, you can either ask the talker to be quiet (if you are close by) or you can raise your hand and share your complaint with the entire room. This should make it perfectly clear to the incessant talker that he needs to pipe down and listen up.

Boasting

"I am Malay (my ethnic group in Malaysia). It is rude for a person to boast about one's achievement to another because it might offend the other person. For example, when a mother talks about how successful her offspring are to another person, the other person might take it differently because her offspring might not be as successful. Mrs. A's son may turn out to be a politician while Mrs. B's son may have dropped out of college or, even worse, become bankrupt. Mrs. B, in response, may keep quiet during the conversation. This scenario is worse if Mrs. A happens to talk really loud on a train where everyone gets to listen about her son. This is my biggest pet peeve."

—*Diba Jamalluddin*

Diba lives in a culture in which modesty is a virtue, and it is a good example of how boasting about ourselves and our loved ones can hurt the feelings of others. *The Solution:* If you are annoyed with someone's boasting, try to change the conversation. First validate that the boaster certainly should be proud of whatever he is sharing. Then, introduce a new topic to the individual or group of people and see if you can divert some of the attention away from the boaster. If this doesn't work, you can politely excuse yourself from the conversation. You don't need to subject yourself to excessive boasting by others.

Names

> "I hate when women call me 'honey,' 'baby,' 'sweetheart,' or some other term of affection! If I called them by any of those terms they would demand my nuts in a jar!"
>
> —*George N. from Orlando, Florida*

Though this assumption may be a little extreme, my suggestion is to first understand that in some cultures, particularly in southern states in the United States, these terms of endearment are not said to irk you, but to be friendly. If it makes you uncomfortable, you're responsible for saying something like, "I would prefer if you would call me George, not 'honey.' I reserve 'sweetheart' for my wife."

> "Forgetting someone's name really annoys me!"
>
> —*Many people*

Most of us have been in this situation: You are in a room and you recognize the person coming toward you as someone you know you have met before. He says hello to you using your name and you can't remember his. ***The Solution:*** The secret is to ask him for it. But make it as nondescript as possible. Say, "I know we met last month and I enjoyed talking with you. Your name is on the tip of my tongue. Please remind me what it is." The other person will be flattered that his name is important to you and will completely understand about your lapse of memory—it happens to him too. Did you know that the only phrase that is common to every language on earth is "your name is on the tip of my tongue"? There isn't a culture on earth in which this is not a common problem.

"I'm bothered when someone forgets my name."

—*Various people*

If you are in the middle of introducing someone you just met to someone else, and you forget a name, ask him for it. More important, don't ignore someone because you have forgotten his name. But what if the person doing the introduction forgets *your* name? ***The Solution:*** Ultimately, it is your responsibility to share it. They might say, "Do you know each other?" That is a huge clue that he can't take the introduction any further so your response would be, "Hello. I am Cynthia Lett from The Lett Group. May I have your name?" or "Hello. I'm Cynthia Lett and it is my first time in Paduka, Kentucky. And you are?"

"I hate it when my name is mispronounced!"

—*Anonymous*

If you have a difficult or unusual name this probably happens to you all the time. ***The Solution:*** It is your responsibility at the moment you hear your name mispronounced to make the correction. Let's say your introducer says, "Cynthia Lett, may I introduce you to Yakim Melomatteo" (and pronounces it "Ya kim" instead of "Ha Keem"). Your responsibility is to reintroduce yourself, saying your name loudly and clearly enough for others to understand the proper pronunciation. You could add, "It is a difficult name," if you don't want to hurt the introducer's feelings, or you could not make any comment about it. Either would be acceptable.

"I intensely dislike people who do not know me and will address me by my first name. The English language does not have a formal and a colloquial way of addressing people. I detest that practice and I am surprised that the habit is so widespread."

—*Dr. Alicia Radice (whose first language is Spanish)*

Americans have the reputation for being overly familiar in our greetings, especially when we first meet someone. Children are taught to address their parents' adult friends by the same name their parents do—the familiar first name. They are also taught to address their teachers by their first name or to think the formal address entails appending Ms. or Mr. to the person's first name. The respect we hope our children will have for adults and strangers is never achieved because they are not taught to use honorifics and family names. It is no wonder that as adults the concept of formal address to others is so difficult and uncomfortable. What do you do if someone you just met automatically addresses you by your first name and you prefer to be called by a more formal title? ***The Solution:*** Just say something. "I prefer Mr. Smith" or "Please call me Mr. Smith" are perfectly appropriate responses. The other person may immediately snicker and say, "Well, aren't we formal?" Never mind what he says. It is your name and if he doesn't respect your wish, he is in the wrong.

> "My name is Margaret May Coleman Lambert. My first name is Margaret May—yes, that is a double first name . . . like Rita Mae, Peggy Sue, or Betty Joe. Even after I explain that to people they still insist on calling me Margaret and entering my name in their computer systems as Margaret M. Lambert. This is very problematic because that is not my legal name. . . . Additionally, to insist on calling someone by another or abbreviated form of their name, especially after having been corrected or requested not to do so, is offensive. It is an insult to a person's parents and family as well as a sign of disrespect and callous disregard of the person."
>
> —*Margaret May C. Lambert*

I understand the frustration Margaret May has when people fill in the wrong name on forms. But the second issue is more important: Our name is the one thing that belongs to us and that we should have complete control over. ***The Solution:*** When you first meet someone, by standards of good etiquette you should refer to the person using an honorific (Mr., Ms., Mrs., Dr., etc.) and his last name. If you want to give out your first name (and you have two of them), indicate this fact. It would be better for you to tell the person you are speaking with upfront (especially when it involves filling out a legal form or insurance information) that you have two first names than wait to be annoyed when the forms aren't correct.

Speaking with Others

Key Complaints

People who say, "uh-huh, uh-huh" after everything you say

People who say meaningless things, in an attempt to make themselves look observant or intelligent

People who talk nonstop in the movie theater, in a meeting, or in class

People who refer to themselves in the third person

"My pet peeve is a person who is self-righteous and has all the answers and the only answers, eliminating an open mind to grow and learn in life. The only person they hurt is themselves by not letting in more of life."

—Reverend Marilyn Redmond

We don't like being around "know-it-alls" because we all want our chance to contribute to the conversation. The person who discounts others' opinions only serves to alienate those with whom he is talking. A wise man once told me that everyone has a story and the fun in life is listening to his story and learning from what he has experienced. It is extremely important to enter into a conversation with someone with the intent to listen and learn. ***The Solution:*** First, calm down. There are just going to be some people in the world who feel they know it all and think everyone else wants to know it as well. These people most likely have a self-esteem issue and should be looked upon with compassion and not annoyance. However, if you happen to know the person really well and you feel this is impeding your ability to continue your relationship with them, try to find a polite way to address this issue. When he starts to argue with you, claiming he knows all the answers, be nice, smile, and tell him that no one can know everything and change the subject.

> "My biggest [annoyance] is individuals who raise their voice or hurry their speech at the first sign of input from another, impeding their participation in the conversation. It really bothers me when they take it to the extreme of jumbling their speech or raising their voice to a noticeably high level to onlookers."
>
> —*Katherine Wenke*

The Solution: Take a deep breath, wait for the hyper speaker to finish, and then say that you appreciate his point of view but that you'd like to have a moment to finish what you were saying or to give your input without interruption.

> "I find it very disrespectful when people gossip about things they have no idea about, especially in front of big groups of people."
>
> —*Megan Sherba*

The Solution: If you are privy to the gossip, tell the gossiper, "I think we should probably not discuss this, as we most likely don't know all the details. This conversation is not professional right now and I think we should change the subject." If this doesn't stop the gossip, leave the conversation.

> "The most irritating peeve I have is people who interrupt, or people who tell someone else's story."
>
> —*Barbara Kracher*

The Solution: Informing the interrupter that you are still speaking (of course using a calm demeanor) will keep him quiet until you have finished. Then, turn to him and ask what he wanted to say.

"My spouse won't believe something I say but then believes it when one of his or her friends says it. How infuriating!"

—Anonymous

We want confirmation that what we say, people believe. But we are so close and so attached to our spouse that our saying something is like having our spouse say it to himself. If the same information came from an outside but trusted source, it becomes more real and thus, believable. ***The Solution:*** Rest assured that it isn't you, it is your partner and be happy that at least someone got the message through to your spouse.

Grammar and Usage

Key Complaints

Improper subject-verb agreement

Misspelled words

Improper enunciation of commonly used words

Saying "people that" did something rather than "people who" did something

Saying "things that are more good" rather than "things that are better"

When I told colleagues that I was going to write this book, many asked if there was going to be a section on English grammar. Because so many examples of poor grammar bother so many people, I figured I had to include a section. The problem is that I am not a grammarian, just someone who has paid attention in elementary grammar and high school writing classes. So in this section, I want to illustrate some common annoyances and overall advice about using correct grammar and usage (both for us and our fellow speakers).

> "I become annoyed with people who say 'I seen it.' You *saw* it, not *seen* it!"
>
> —*LaTaunia N. Crockett*

In addition to this annoyance, several contributors shared that saying "axe him" instead of "ask him" bothers them. Additionally, these examples were cited:

POlice instead of poLICE—emphasis on the "o" instead of the "eese"

The Solution: Though modeling good grammar and usage is important when we speak with others, it is also worth noting that using the word "axe" instead of "ask" is not necessarily improper—it is basically a different way of speaking (more properly termed as Ebonics or African-American English). It is true that this word does not necessarily mean "ask" in the English dictionary, but we need to be careful when confronting someone about the language he or she uses. Take into consideration where the person is from and use your best judgment when contemplating correcting their speech.

> "In formal and informal correspondence, it is essential to use proper grammar. For instance, avoid starting conversations or written paragraphs with 'I' or any variation of the personal pronoun. Also do not begin any written sentence with the word 'there.' Also, the word 'irregardless' shouldn't be spoken or written because the word doesn't exist in Webster's dictionary. As well, there is no percentage greater than 100—100 percent indicates *all* of something and one cannot have more than *all* of anything. One can have twice or three times the amount of product, fun, success, etc., but there really is no percent over 100."
>
> —*Kerri*

Kerri brings up a lot of good grammar and usage points. These may be important to know when writing formal correspondence or academic papers, but some of these ways of starting sentences or speaking are casual and should be given some leeway on our part during casual conversation. The word "irregardless" is now a word in Webster's dictionary (however with an explanation that it is still not generally accepted). Furthermore, the colloquialism "giving 110 percent" is an exaggeration, but because it isn't technically accurate, it does annoy grammarians and wordsmiths. **The Solution:** It is actually bad etiquette to correct others' grammatical errors, so it would be best to just shrug it off as commonly used English faux pas. If someone asks for your opinion on their grammer then you are free to share what you know.

> "[I'm annoyed by] poor spelling and the use of site vs. cite."
>
> —*Maida S.*

It's true that you cannot "site" anything. The word comes from the Latin for *citation*. **The Solution:** If you encounter someone misspelling a word in a paper, e-mail, or other written correspondence, use your judgment about how well you know the person and, if you feel comfortable, just give him a friendly reminder of how to spell the word correctly.

> "People who stress the wrong syllable in certain words are obnoxious."
>
> —*Anonymous*

As I mentioned before, I don't pretend to be a wordsmith or professional grammarian so to explain the most common perceived faux pas in speech, I have asked Robert Beard, PhD, author of *The Hundred Funniest Words in English,* to allow me to share what he wrote on his Web site alphadictionary.com:

"I recently heard an NPR reporter misplace the accent on a word and it reminded me of the invisible suffix in English. I did not write down the specific word (I've heard this error many times on radio and

TV) but it was a word like *survey,* which is pronounced both *sur***vey** and **sur***vey.* Both are legitimate words. Do you know the rule which governs where the accent falls? Here are some more examples:

re**ject** : **re**ject

in**crease** : **in**crease

sub**ject**: **sub**ject

If you think the accent on the second syllable indicates a verb and accent on the initial syllable indicates a noun—you're right."

So, if you happen to hear someone emphasizing the incorrect syllable, what should you do? ***The Solution:*** Kindly correct the person you are talking to by repeating what he said (showing yourself as an "active listener") and then stressing the correct syllable. This will not only teach the person the correct pronunciation but will convey that you were listening intently to what he said.

> "I am annoyed when people use the words 'someone'
> or 'a person' then use the pronoun "they" as though the
> words were plural."
>
> —*Lorna Hemp Boll*

    The Solution: Kindly correct his language usage if it is in written form. Otherwise, is it really that necessary to get annoyed by this when you can obviously understand what the person means by the context of his words?

> "The diminished use of the plural in the English language
> is disconcerting."
>
> —*Anonymous*

Many people who complain about the decline of the English language are perfectionists who have a stronger knowledge than I do of the reasons why speech is often difficult to listen to and understand. A common irritation is using the plural number in English. English traditionally distinguishes one or more objects by a distinct plural, e.g., one table, two tables, many tables. Lately, however, problems have arisen in the language that suggest this plural distinction is in trouble.

For example, you may have heard people say things like: "A *large amount* of birds flew by" or "We found *less weapons* than we expected." The English language once distinguished nouns referring to substances that are always in the singular by using amounts for singular substances and numbers for countable objects in the plural:

A *large amount* of Kool-Aid, ambition, coffee, or crawfish gumbo; A *large number* of pigeons, bullwhips, armadillos, or blueberry pies.

The same distinction was made by *less* and *fewer*. *Less* was used only if the noun was uncountable: *less* Kool-Aid, *less* coffee, *less* crawfish gumbo. *Fewer* was applied to countable objects: *fewer* bullwhips, *fewer* armadillos, and *fewer* blueberry pies. This distinction, too, seems to be flying out the window these days. It is difficult to listen to this "new" kind of English, but could this be a natural evolution in the course of modern English?

One final bit of evidence: Kay Bock, one of the nation's leading psycholinguists, has been researching the plurals of nouns and finds that we are confusing singular with plural more and more. In English, the noun that is the subject of a sentence agrees with its verb. Roughly, if the noun has the plural "s" on it, the verb doesn't (The pigs *run)* but if the noun doesn't have one (is singular), the verb does (The pig *runs)*. What Professor Bock is finding is that agreement is not always between the subject (noun) and the verb, as grammar dictates, but between the noun nearest the verb, whatever its function in the sentence. For example:

A rootery of pigs were running through the barnyard. As the problem of rooting pigs grow, we have to address them.

In these sentences, the subject nouns are group and problem, so the verb should contain the -s:

A *rootery* of pigs *was* running through the barnyard.

As the *problem* of rooting pigs *grows,* we have to address it.

Bock thinks language is changing but such sentences sound a lot like bad grammar to those who have studied the proper "rules" of the English language.

Before summing up, let me alert you to one final error that seems to fit the pattern of the three above. To understand it, you have to be

> For Your Information: this has nothing to do with the difference between British and U.S. English, where the British use the plural with what linguists call "collective nouns" (as opposed to U.S. English use of *rootery* above): nouns that are singular in form but refer to a plurality of objects:
>
> The Parliament are in session.
>
> The crew are on alert.
>
> The team play well together.
>
> The British are consistent in this usage. In the United States it seems that our grasp of the rules concerning plurality is diminishing and, if this is the case, we could see the plural disappear from the language in a relative short linguistic period—perhaps, fewer than 200 years!

aware of another loss in English: The number of suffixes for marking grammatical functions, such as numbers, people, and tenses, are quickly disappearing. Suffixes such as -dom, -ery, -ess and many others are no longer being added to new words. The result of this is that the suffixes we are left with have to serve more and more functions. For example, the suffix -s is used to mark the following:

The plural: ant-s, launching-s, door-s *The third singular present tense of verbs:* He/she/it run-s, smell-s, plunge-s *Making nouns out of adjectives:* linguistic-s, acrobatic-s, mathematic-s *Possessive:* George's, Bush's, the anaconda's

This brings us to the fourth bit of evidence that at least U.S. English-speakers are losing their grasp of the plural: Plural numbers are often confused with nonplural uses. You have probably heard things such as this said:

Boscov's are having a big sale this week.

Logistics are not my forte.

These would be merely speech errors if they didn't fit the pattern created by the first three bits of evidence: We are losing our grip on the plural of words. So, how will we be able to communicate if the plural disappears? Would you believe that many languages get away without the singular-plural distinction today and have been doing so for millennia? Oriental languages like Vietnamese and Chinese have no singular-plural distinction at all. The reason these languages do without plural numbers suggests that it might be redundant in English: We generally use the plural with some modifier that makes the word's plural nature obvious.

Many Cadillacs	Many Cadillac
Five toads	Five toad
A few warts	A few wart

Do we really need -s when we already have many, five, or few in the sentence? The Chinese and Vietnamese have built advanced civilizations on languages limited to phrases like those in the second column. English could become more like Chinese!

The Ultimate Solution: If the English language is abandoning the plural, it is still too early to be sure. However, if the process has begun, there is no stopping it, so tormenting your kids with constant grammatical corrections will not work. Only time will tell and, as we all know, time takes its time.

Bonus Fun: Misinterpretations

These misinterpretations from native tongues into English are fun to read and allow us to understand that we all do our best to communicate across cultures but when we make a mistake that is apparent to the reader or listener, but not the source of the communication, our humanity must allow us to laugh privately and correct what should be corrected to avoid further embarrassment. Over the years I have collected these gems. Perhaps you too have seen them posted in your travels.

In Western Europe:

• Cocktail lounge, Norway: LADIES ARE REQUESTED NOT TO HAVE CHILDREN IN THE BAR.

- Airline ticket office, Copenhagen: WE TAKE YOUR BAGS AND SEND THEM IN ALL DIRECTIONS.
- Hotel in Vienna: IN CASE OF FIRE, DO YOUR UTMOST TO ALARM THE HOTEL PORTER.
- At a Budapest zoo: PLEASE DO NOT FEED THE ANIMALS. IF YOU HAVE ANY SUITABLE FOOD, GIVE IT TO THE GUARD ON DUTY.
- Hotel lobby, Bucharest: THE LIFT IS BEING FIXED FOR THE NEXT DAY. DURING THAT TIME WE REGRET THAT YOU WILL BE UNBEARABLE.
- Doctor's office, Rome: SPECIALIST IN WOMEN AND OTHER DISEASES.
- A laundry in Rome: LADIES, LEAVE YOUR CLOTHES HERE AND SPEND THE AFTERNOON HAVING A GOOD TIME.
- In an Italian cemetery: PERSONS ARE PROHIBITED FROM PICKING FLOWERS FROM ANY BUT THEIR OWN GRAVES.
- Hotel brochure, Italy: THIS HOTEL IS RENOWNED FOR ITS PEACE AND SOLITUDE. IN FACT, CROWDS FROM ALL OVER THE WORLD FLOCK HERE TO ENJOY ITS SOLITUDE.
- In a Swiss Mountain inn: SPECIAL TODAY—NO ICE CREAM.
- On the menu of a Swiss restaurant: OUR WINES LEAVE YOU NOTHING TO HOPE FOR.
- A sign posted in Germany's Black Forest: IT IS STRICTLY FORBIDDEN ON OUR BLACK FOREST CAMPING SITE THAT PEOPLE OF DIFFERENT SEX, FOR INSTANCE, MEN AND WOMEN, LIVE TOGETHER IN ONE TENT UNLESS THEY ARE MARRIED WITH EACH OTHER FOR THIS PURPOSE.
- A sign seen on an automatic restroom hand dryer in Germany: DO NOT ACTIVATE WITH WET HANDS.
- On the grounds of a private school in Scotland: NO TRESPASSING WITHOUT PERMISSION.
- Hotel elevator, Paris: PLEASE LEAVE YOUR VALUES AT THE FRONT DESK.

In Eastern Europe:

- Hotel, Yugoslavia: THE FLATTENING OF UNDERWEAR WITH PLEASURE IS THE JOB OF THE CHAMBERMAID.
- In the lobby of a Moscow hotel across from a Russian Orthodox monastery: YOU ARE WELCOME TO VISIT THE CEMETERY WHERE

FAMOUS RUSSIAN AND SOVIET COMPOSERS, ARTISTS, AND WRITERS ARE BURIED DAILY EXCEPT THURSDAY.

- Hotel catering to skiers, Austria: NOT TO PERAMBULATE THE CORRIDORS IN THE HOURS OF REPOSE IN THE BOOTS OF ASCENSION.
- Taken from a menu, Poland: SALAD A FIRM'S OWN MAKE; LIMPID RED BEET SOUP WITH CHEESY DUMPLINGS IN THE FORM OF A FINGER; ROASTED DUCK LET LOOSE; BEEF RASHERS BEATEN IN THE COUNTRY PEOPLE'S FASHION.
- From the *Soviet Weekly*: HERE WILL BE A MOSCOW EXHIBITION OF ARTS BY 15,000 SOVIET REPUBLIC PAINTERS AND SCULPTORS. THESE WERE EXECUTED OVER THE PAST TWO YEARS.
- On the door of a Moscow hotel room: IF THIS IS YOUR FIRST VISIT TO THE USSR, YOU ARE WELCOME TO IT.
- Tourist agency, Czechoslovakia: TAKE ONE OF OUR HORSE-DRIVEN CITY TOURS. WE GUARANTEE NO MISCARRIAGES.

Australia and New Zealand

- On a poster in Sydney: ARE YOU AN ADULT THAT CANNOT READ? IF SO, WE CAN HELP.
- In a New Zealand restaurant: OPEN SEVEN DAYS A WEEK, AND WEEKENDS TOO.
- On a highway sign in Australia: TAKE NOTICE: WHEN THIS SIGN IS UNDER WATER; THIS ROAD IS IMPASSABLE.

In Asia

- In 2002, a sign in front of a rock garden in the Forbidden City in Beijing warned tourists: PLEASE DO NOT CLIMB THE ROCKETRY.
- Sign over the information booth in a Beijing railroad station: QUESTION AUTHORITY.
- Included with the package of complimentary wares in a Chinese hotel was a pair of workout shorts marked: UNCOMPLIMENTARY PANTS.

- A paragliding site near Beijing has a sign that reads: SITE OF JUMPING UMBRELLA.
- The translation of the Ethnic Minorities Park in Beijing for a long time was RACIST PARK.
- Supermarket, Hong Kong: FOR YOUR CONVENIENCE, WE RECOMMEND COURTEOUS, EFFICIENT SELF-SERVICE.
- An advertisement by a Hong Kong dentist: TEETH EXTRACTED BY THE LATEST METHODISTS.
- The box of a clockwork toy made in Hong Kong: GUARANTEED TO WORK. THROUGHOUT ITS USEFUL LIFE.
- Booklet about using a hotel air conditioner, Japan: COOLES AND HEATES; IF YOU WANT CONDITION OF WARM AIR IN YOUR ROOM, PLEASE CONTROL YOURSELF.
- Translated from Japanese to English and included in the instructions for a soap bubble gun: WHILE SOLUTION IS NOT TOXIC IT WILL NOT MAKE CHILD EDIBLE.
- Tokyo hotel's rules and regulations: GUESTS ARE REQUESTED NOT TO SMOKE OR DO OTHER DISGUSTING BEHAVIORS IN BED.
- Hotel, Japan: YOU ARE INVITED TO TAKE ADVANTAGE OF THE CHAMBERMAID.
- Car rental brochure, Tokyo: WHEN PASSENGER OF FOOT HEAVE IN SIGHT, TOOTLE THE HORN. TRUMPET HIM MELODIOUSLY AT FIRST, BUT IF HE STILL OBSTACLES YOUR PASSAGE THEN TOOTLE HIM WITH VIGOUR.
- Hotel room notice, Chiang-Mai, Thailand: PLEASE DO NOT BRING SOLICITORS INTO YOUR ROOM.

In Africa

- In an East African newspaper: A NEW SWIMMING POOL IS RAPIDLY TAKING SHAPE SINCE THE CONTRACTORS HAVE THROWN IN THE BULK OF THEIR WORKERS.
- In a Nairobi restaurant: CUSTOMERS WHO FIND OUR WAITRESSES RUDE OUGHT TO SEE THE MANAGER.

- On a South African building: MENTAL HEALTH PREVENTION CENTRE.
- In a South African maternity ward: NO CHILDREN ALLOWED.

In Mexico and South America

- Hotel, Acapulco: THE MANAGER HAS PERSONALLY PASSED ALL THE WATER SERVED HERE.
- In a restaurant window: DON'T STAND THERE AND BE HUNGRY. COME ON IN AND GET FED UP.

CONCLUSION

In the end, whether we are bothered by others' behavior or not is solely our decision. Getting along with others, especially those we live with or work with, is a constant give and take. Remember, others are trying their best to get along with you and overlook *your* annoying habits. It is easier if we like the other person, even easier if we love him. But it is not always easy.

When other people's habits bother me, I believe that I have been presented with an opportunity to practice tolerance and patience. We never get good at something without a lot of practice. Empathy is also important in helping you to understand that others are not out to ruin your day. Many people act out what they are feeling. Our feelings come from our personal reactions to things that are going on in our lives. Everyone has bad days. Everyone has challenges in life that others will never know about. Everyone has to learn how to get along better with others. You haven't learned all the lessons yet—neither have I. When presented with a common annoyance of mine, the first thing I say to myself is, "Things may be difficult for them today and they are not paying attention to how others feel." I also know that rarely is someone's behavior personally directed at me. I just happen to be there and if I don't like what the person is doing, I have the power to ignore the situation or person, or to get up and leave.

Most people don't know when they have done something to offend or bother you. They don't know because rarely do we say anything—we just simmer in our frustration and anger. Instead, request in the most compassionate and kind manner you have that they please stop. We need to learn to teach others how to treat us; we must also train ourselves to react more positively toward others' annoying behaviors. After all, most of the world's population have never taken an etiquette class or read this book.

RESOURCES

AAA Foundation for Traffic Safety, "Aggressive Driving: Three Studies." Washington, D.C., 1997.

Tavris, Carol. *Anger: The Misunderstood Emotion.* Simon & Schuster, NY, 1989.

O'Connor, James V. Cuss Control. The Complete Book on How to Curb Your Cursing. iUniverse, April, 2000.

Beard, Robert. *The Hundred Funniest Words in English.* Lexiteria, 2009. www.alphadictionary.com and www.lexiteria.com

Sutton, Robert I The No Asshole Rule: Building a Civilized Workplace and Surviving One That Isn't," Grand Central Publishing, 2007.

Cenedella, Mark. "The 'F' Word Means You're Fired!" Ladders.co.uk, April 28, 2008.

Chao, Loretta. "Rise in Office Rudeness Weighs on Productivity, Retention." *The Wall Street Journal,* January 17, 2006.

24-Karat Etiquette

Golden Rules from the World's Most Glamorous Zip Code

by Lisa Gaché

In Beverly Hills, fame and wealth can buy everything—except class, grace, and sophistication. In *24 Karat Etiquette*, Lisa Gaché offers a behind-the-scenes look at Beverly Hills residents' unique social dilemmas through the eyes of an etiquette expert. From Saudi princesses to Oscar winners, talent agents to intelligence operatives, child actresses, butlers, and football players, Lisa has amassed an astounding roster. In this book, she reflects on those experiences to teach you how to present yourself as a respectable professional in real-world situations, whether you're located in 90210, 10001, or anywhere in between.

In today's technological world, Lisa counsels clients on more than table manners. Thanks to the explosion of social media, netiquette is a vital new discipline. You'll learn how to send emails, texts, and messages on a variety of different social media outlets, as well as how to manage your online profiles to show yourself in the best light possible.

$22.95 Hardcover • ISBN 978-1-62636-169-0

ALSO AVAILABLE

The Official Book of Electronic Etiquette

by Charles Winters, Anne Winters, Elizabeth Anne Winters, and Charles Winters II

Whether you are sending an email, tweeting, or just wondering if it's appropriate to answer your phone, here are the answers to all your communication questions. Covering phones, the Internet, television, and much, much more, this accessible and lively handbook provides up-to-date information on all your modern electronic needs. Written by the founders of the National League of Junior Cotillions, this book provides the reader with access to information sought after by hundreds of people. With an easy question and answer format and a full, comprehensive index, *The Official Book of Electronic Etiquette* is a necessity for everyone who wants to know right from wrong in the electronic age.

$14.95 Hardcover • ISBN 978-1-61608-102-7

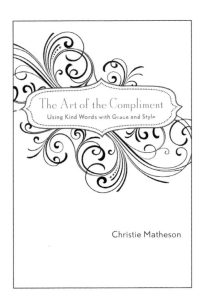

Art of the Compliment

Using Kind Words with Grace and Style

by Christie Matheson

A few well-chosen words can elicit smiles, inspire happiness, transform moods, and turn a bad day into a good one. Philosopher William James once said, "The deepest principle in human nature is the desire to be appreciated." This is a fun, fabulous, reader-friendly book all about compliments—the history of compliments, how to use them, best-loved compliments, and how to take them.

$14.95 Hardcover • ISBN 978-1-60239-636-4

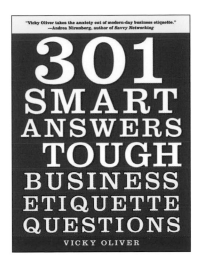

301 Smart Answers to Tough Business Etiquette Questions

by Vicky Oliver

301 Smart Answers to Tough Business Etiquette Questions has the answers you need to survive daily life in the professional environment. Following the same popular Q&A format of her bestselling *301 Smart Answers to Tough Interview Questions*, Oliver will tell you how to get the job and how to keep it by navigating all the intricacies of the modern workplace.

Etiquette is not a throwback to some bygone age, but has a direct and tangible impact on your career right here and now. Off come the white gloves as Oliver tears away the corporate veil to reveal things they still don't teach at Harvard Business School, such as:

- Making a good first impression (and how to fix a bad one!)
- How to behave in elevators, airplanes, and supply closets
- Surviving cabs, commutes, and coffee shops
- Why time is not necessarily money everywhere on the planet
- Pre-approved conversational topics from A to Z
- Dining rules and regulations for the twenty-first century
- What to do when you are suddenly unemployed
- Electronic communication
- And much more!

301 Smart Answers to Tough Business Etiquette Questions will ensure that you know how to conduct yourself in every conceivable professional interaction.

$12.95 Paperback • ISBN 978-1-61608-141-6

Look, Speak, & Behave for Women

Expert Advice on Image, Etiquette, and Effective
Communication for the Professional

by Jamie Yasko-Mangum, C.I.C.

For years, highly paid executives at major corporations have had the benefit of professional image consultants to give them feedback about their presentation in the workplace. That expert advice has helped them to dress properly for any business occasion, improve their public speaking and presentation skills, understand the dos and don'ts of the workplace, and enhance their standing in the business community. Now that same type of guidance is available to anyone—recent graduates looking to enter the workplace as well as managers and executives looking to polish themselves and their skills. Jamie Yasko-Mangum's clients include Estée Lauder, the American Management Association, Pfizer, Darden Restaurants, high schools, colleges, and universities. They hire her to give seminars to employees and students on how to project a positive and smart self-image, create a polished appearance, understand what is and is not proper behavior, and see how to communicate intelligently. Readers will find ideas for improving their credibility, authority, reputation, and confidence in a workplace environment, regardless of their profession or position.

$19.95 Hardcover • ISBN 978-1-60239-026-3

Look, Speak, & Behave for Men

Expert Advice on Image, Etiquette, and Effective
Communication for the Professional

by Jamie Yasko-Mangum, C.I.C.

For years, highly paid executives at major corporations have had the benefit of
professional image consultants to give them feedback about their presentation
in the workplace. That expert advice has helped them to dress properly
for any business occasion, improve their public speaking and presentation
skills, understand the dos and don'ts of the workplace, and enhance their
standing in the business community. Now that same type of guidance is
available to anyone—recent graduates looking to enter the workplace as
well as managers and executives looking to polish themselves and their
skills. Jamie Yasko-Mangum's clients include Estée Lauder, the American
Management Association, Pfizer, Darden Restaurants, high schools, colleges,
and universities. They hire her to give seminars to employees and students on
how to project a positive and smart self-image, create a polished appearance,
understand what is and is not proper behavior, and see how to communicate
intelligently. Readers will find ideas for improving their credibility, authority,
reputation, and confidence in a workplace environment, regardless of their
profession or position.

$19.95 Hardcover • ISBN 978-1-60239-025-6

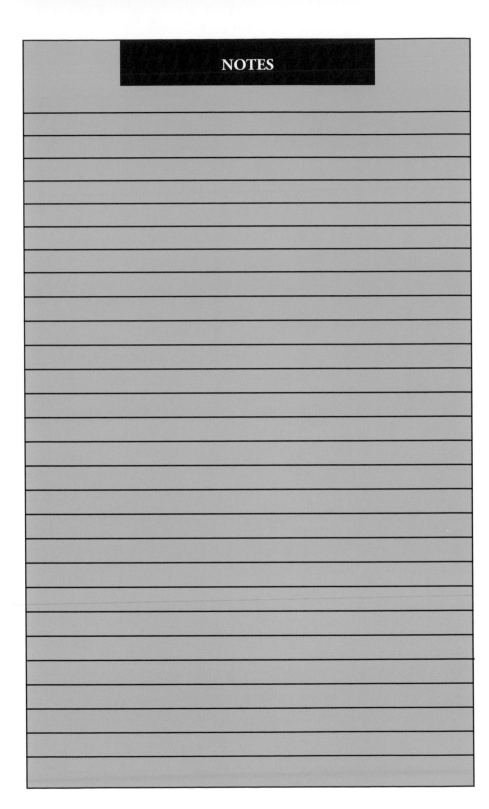

NOTES

NOTES

NOTES

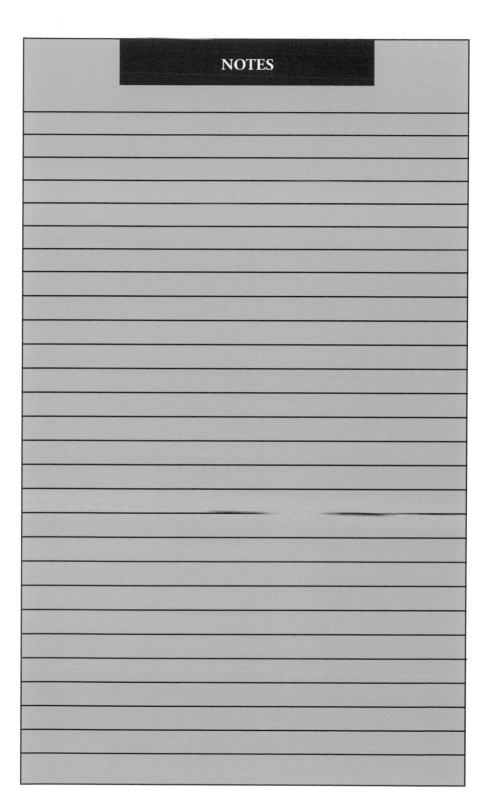

NOTES

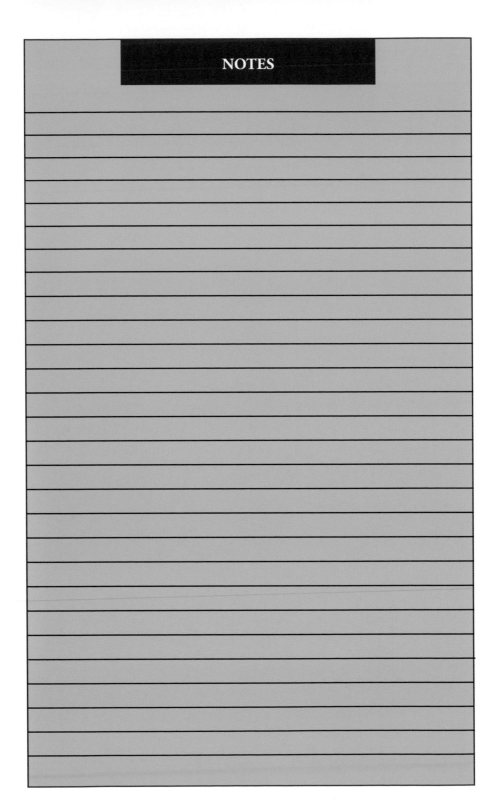

NOTES

NOTES

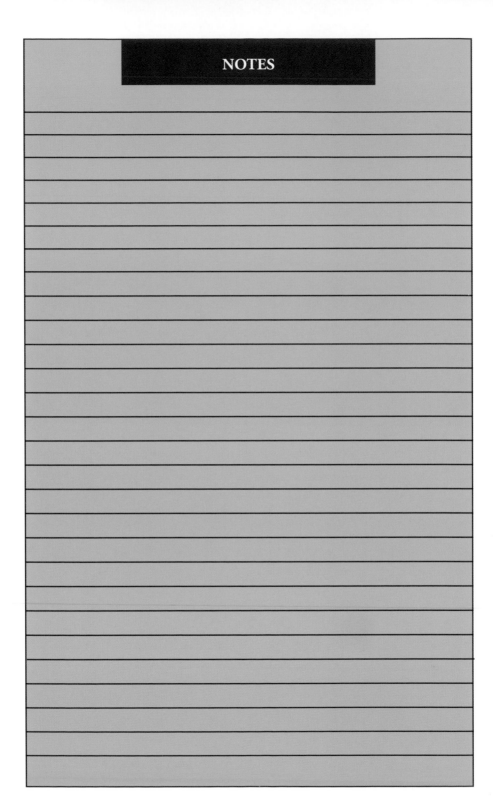

NOTES

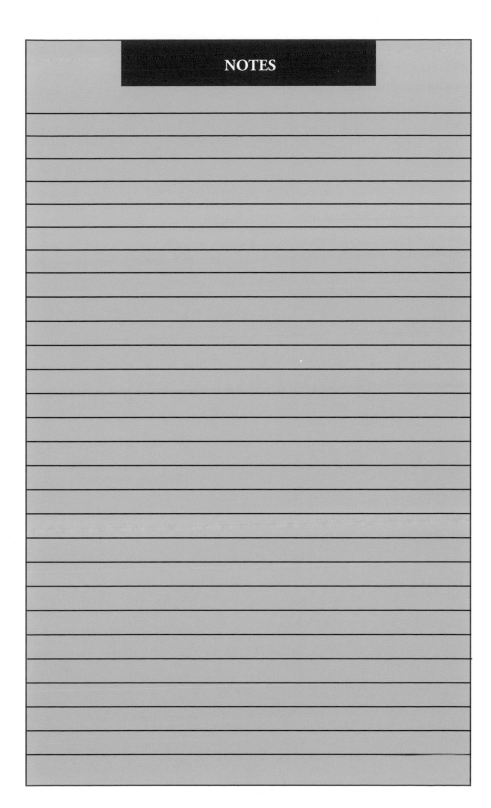

NOTES

NOTES

NOTES

NOTES

NOTES

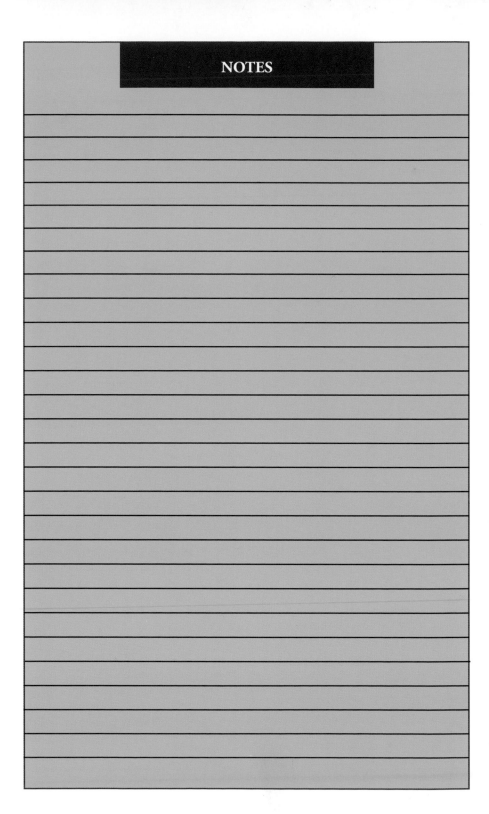

NOTES